SHADOW
IN MY
MIND

SHADOW
IN MY
MIND
GHOSTS OF VIET NAM

Tony Stephens

Outskirts Press, Inc.
Denver, Colorado

SHADOW IN MY MIND
GHOSTS OF VIET NAM

Outskirts Press, Inc.
http://www.outskirtspress.com

ISBN: 978-1-4327-4086-3

Outskirts Press and the "OP" logo are trademarks belonging to Outskirts Press, Inc.

PRINTED IN THE UNITED STATES OF AMERICA

11 October 1996

I am starting to write some things down that I may never finish nor allow anyone to ever read about my life and my experiences in Viet Nam.

Before I get started, a little about my life growing up. We grew up believing that we were poor, but we really weren't. Actually, I had things a lot better than my older brothers and sisters because they grew up during the "Great Depression". When they were young, my family roamed around and my dad found work where ever he could. They lived in shacks or tents or whatever was available. Someone once asked my older sister whether or not she had read the book "The Grapes of Rath". She replied "read it hell, we lived it!! By the time I came along my Dad was a "sharecropper" and rented a lot of farmland. I was the last child of an even dozen!! We stayed in one place after I was born and rented land from the same person. There were only nine kids alive after I was born, because three children had died before I was born. My older siblings said that two of them were buried in the back yard somewhere in Arizona.

I know that God had a reason for putting me on this earth. When I was born, my mother had already had eleven kids. My brother just older than me did not live. After the old country doctor delivered my brother, he told my mom that her body couldn't take any more. He told her to go home and rest up for six weeks and then come back to see him. He had scheduled her for a hysterectomy at the end of the six weeks. She came back to have the hysterectomy and found out that she was pregnant with me!!! Talk about coming in just under the wire. That is how close I came to not being born.

The older kids told me of how hard my dad was raised, so he raised us hard. They said his mother was mean and cruel to him. Besides the awful hard work from daylight to dark, sometimes the way he treated us bordered on cruel and sadistic. I have been beaten with everything that is laying loose on a farm, from 2x4's, to fan belts, to trace chains to shovel handles. We worked hard, but we always had something to eat, because we raised most of what we ate. We butchered our own beef, pork and chickens. We also grew everything we ate so my mom only bought staples like salt, flour and sugar. She made all of our shirts from the chicken feed and flour sacks.

There must have been some good times growing up, but I mostly remember the bad ones because there were more of them!! One time (of many), that I remember, I was forking back cotton in an old wooden trailer while my dad drove the cotton stripper. The old two-row stripper transferred the cotton from the stalks through an elevator and dumped it in the front of the trailer. I had to throw the cotton to the back of the trailer to keep it from falling out the front of the trailer. I got caught up so I decided to climb up on the elevator of the stripper and ride on top of it. The elevator was about ten feet above the front of the trailer. The front of the trailer was broken and all splintered from the elevator hitting it while turning around at the end of the rows. The tractor hit a ditch washed out by rain and bounced the elevator so hard, I fell off. I landed on the splintered boards of the trailer right in the middle of my back, and then fell to the ground, (another seven feet). Just as I hit the ground, my dad looked around and saw me. He slammed on the brakes to avoid running over me with the trailer and dismounted the tractor. I was in excruciating pain and my back was bleeding. I thought my dad was coming to check to see if I was hurt, but instead, he bent over and pulled up a handful of cotton stalks and began beating me with them!! When he whipped you, he didn't just hit your rear end, he hit you all over. He beat the blood out of my naked arms and even whipped my already bleeding back. He told me to get back inside that trailer and see if I could work the way I was supposed to. I was eleven years old at that time.

As I said, he worked us really hard, but maybe it made us better men when we grew up. Some of the things he did to us were cruel mentally and that was about as bad as the physical abuse. Numerous times throughout my childhood, he would cuss us and tell us how worthless we were, but that if we would get a certain amount of work done by noon on Saturday, he would take us to town. We lived thirteen miles out in the country. He always assigned us more work than we could possibly get done in that length of time. But, we would always try. We worked our guts out from daylight to dark, sometimes sixteen and eighteen hours a day. Then on Saturday morning, we would hit the fields well before sun up, then around midmorning it appeared as though we just might be able to get all the work done by noon.

"Every damn time" he told us this, around ten or eleven o'clock, we would look up and see the dust cloud behind his pickup going to town. He had lied to us again and was leaving us in the fields while he went to town. Just one more reason we felt the way we did. He probably expected it or knew that we would stop working for the rest of that day, but we did. We would stop whatever we were working on and go swimming down on the river or find something to do, anything but work. One of my brothers use to "jimmy" the tractor so it wouldn't run. That way, he would have an excuse for not working any more. I didn't need an excuse, I was mad as hell.

We couldn't go hunting, because we had no money to buy ammunition. Once I found my dad's twenty-two shells and shot them all. He nearly beat me to death!! We never went fishing; there were no ponds or lakes within walking distance from our house. We usually just went down in the pasture and played some type of games we made up. We did anything we could to take our minds off what was really bothering us.

Christmas has never been a fond memory for me. To this

day, I just can't get into the Christmas Spirit. My wife loves that time of the year, and I feel really bad that I ruin it for her, but I just can't. I was always lucky or fortunate if I ever got more than one gift for Christmas. Sometimes I didn't even get one. I knew times were hard, but my nephews and cousins always got loads of gifts. When I was seven or eight, I got a new leather belt for my one gift. I remember my nephews got twenty-one gifts each (I know because I counted each one as I watched them open them). As I watched them open all those great toys and new clothes, I remember saying something under my breath about how unfair I thought it was. My dad heard me and jerked me up by one arm and beat me something awful with my new belt, then took his pocketknife and cut it into three pieces then threw the pieces out into the yard.

When I was ten, I hit the jackpot. I got a new Daisy Red Ryder BB gun. Two of my nephews got one too. We all went down to the barn and shot at birds, tin cans etc. As luck would have it, someone shot a window in the house. It only made a little round snowflake looking crack in the window, but that was all the excuse my dad needed. For some reason he was convinced that I was the one who shot the window (and it could have been me). He didn't say a word about it until my nephews went home. Then he gave me a good cussing. He called us names that cut us to our very souls. He had a way of telling us how sorry and worthless we were over and over, almost every day of our lives.

He took my BB gun and held it by the barrel and beat me to the ground with the stock, then beat the gun to pieces and wrapped the barrel of it around a porch post. Later, I gathered up the pieces and kept them for a long time. I tried to straighten the barrel, but couldn't. After I was grown, one of my sisters said that sometimes when I didn't get anything for Christmas, she would take the names of her boys off a gift and put my name on it so I would have a gift to open.

Another one of my nephews, in fact two more came to live

with us when I was six or seven. I loved them like little brothers. I guess my dad loved them too, because he treated one of them the way a man should treat his children. I stood back many times and watched my dad hold my nephew and bounce him on his knee. I never remember my dad whipping him or cussing him for any reason. My nephew got lots of gifts and if he wanted something, anything at all, he only had to ask my dad and he got it. My nephew even got us our first television, because he wanted it. One time my dad bought him a really neat pedal car, but I wasn't allowed to ride it. I had one bicycle in my lifetime, but I built it from old ones I found in the trash at the dump ground. It never had rubber tires on it. It would leave two tracks in the dirt where the rims went. I rode that thing for miles on the old dirt roads.

My grandpa lived with us until he died. My grandmother died before I was born. He was my dad's dad. Our old house was small, so I slept with my grandpa and my two brothers slept together in a different bed. We all slept in the same bedroom, but in two different beds. Early one morning when I was about eight, my grandpa woke me up scratching me on the leg really hard. I jumped up and tried to wake him, but couldn't. I ran into my parent's room and woke them. I will always remember yelling, "Come quick, grandpa is dying or going crazy, or something"!!!! It scared me something awful. That stuck in my mind for a long time. My grandpa died a few minutes after that. I guess he must have known he was dying when he scratched my leg. I really loved my grandpa. I sat on the porch and talked to him for hours, something I never did with my dad. I never sat on his lap, because I thought I was too big for that. I do remember grandpa would hug me or put his arm around my shoulder after one of the beatings, or when I was sick. He had no teeth, so sometimes, he would touch his chin to the tip of his nose to make me laugh or take my mind off things.

Other than this grandpa, I only saw my other grandparents two or three times in my life. My dad wouldn't take my mother to see her parents. I know that hurt my mom, but she never complained. When I was twenty-seven years old, I had no grandparents alive and both my parents had passed away. I have friends who still have at least one of their parents today, and we are sixty-four!!

Life was like that for all of us, I guess. Until I left home for good when I was barely seventeen, I felt like a slave. I grew up my whole life, believing with all my heart that I hated my father, at times. That is a terrible thing to say, I know, but I did. Some of the other kids say they felt the same way, but I guess deep down, we really didn't. I know if I did, I didn't hate him when he died, or at least I forgave him for the way he treated me. I never understood and still don't, how a man could treat his own kids that way if he really did love them. I never believed for a moment that he loved me, he couldn't have. I was always convinced that he hated my guts. He must have to treat me that way. He never touched me one single time in my whole life except to beat me. I know that sounds preposterous, but it is the God's Truth. Not once, did he ever hug me, or pat me on the back. I never remember him touching me in a loving way or holding me in his lap when I was very small. I believe that the main reason I couldn't get past the feeling that he didn't love me was my friends' fathers. All my friend's dads always joked around with them and hugged them and wrestled with them. They went hunting and fishing with their dads all the time. The only nonviolent, physical contact, I remember was the day I came home from Viet Nam. He shook my hand and had tears in his eyes. When I think of him, I do my best to believe in my heart that he did love me, but that he just didn't know how to show it.

My mother, on the other hand, was the exact opposite of my dad. If ever there was an angel on this earth, it was my mother. She was the kindest, most loving, giving and caring person on God's Green Earth. She loved everybody and if she ever uttered a bad word about another human, I never heard her. I think she was afraid of my dad, the same as we were. She seldom ever disagreed with him or talked back to him. She worked in the fields, milked cows, fed animals and every thing we had to do. She also raised a houseful of kids of her own along with grand kids, nieces and nephews and did all the housework, cooking, cleaning, clothes mending and doctoring. She never complained, not even when she was sick or worried about something. I remember brushing her hair while standing behind her chair. She loved to have her hair brushed. I will always regret not doing more to help her while growing up.

She did all of this for my whole life, growing up, and never had running water inside our house and no indoor bathroom. We hauled our water and emptied it into a "sistern". This was a hole we dug about twenty feet deep, and then cemented the walls and floor of it. We would "draw" the water up with a bucket, on a pulley and rope, then carry it into the house to drink and use for all other things. Until I started bathing outside by the horse tank, we heated buckets of water on the stove and bathed in a number three washtub. We brought it inside and sat it in the middle of the kitchen floor.

When we were teenagers, my brother and I found an old metal tank. We hoisted it up onto the rungs of the windmill. We fixed it so that the water could be pumped up to it by the windmill. The sun would heat it during the day while we were working in the fields. That thing was great. For the first time in our lives, we could take a hot shower at night. Sometimes, when the temperature reached over one hundred degrees for days, the water felt like it would scald us, but it beat nothing. We had an "outhouse" for a toilet. I never had an indoor bathroom or running water in the house until I moved away from home, and I was the youngest. My mother was a wonderful person and I challenge any person on earth to find anyone who has a bad word to say about her. I loved her with all my heart and soul.

I left home for good when I was barely seventeen. I got a job and started a family of my own. I missed my mom, but oh God how good it felt to get away from the misery we grew up in. I was my own boss now, and I never looked back. The next man, that ever tries to beat me or cuss me, had better go ahead and kill me.

I love my children with all my heart. I raised them with a firm hand, and with rules and discipline but I always tried to be fair. If they needed a whipping, they got it but never a beating like I got. I didn't have to whip them very many times in their entire lives. They were good kids, and still are. I tried to instill a feeling of self-pride in all of them. I taught them to never disrespect their elders, never take something that wasn't theirs, and Heaven help them if they every lied to me. I tried to teach them that "everything has a place" and if they use something, to put it back where it belongs. One thing they still remember is that when they leave a room they are to "turn out the light"!

These "weirdoes" and degenerates we read about and see on TV, that hurt their children, (or any children for that matter) because they had a "bad childhood" need to be hung. They say that because they were mistreated as a child, or had a bad childhood, it caused them to mutilate or torture their own kids. That is a stupid cop-out. If that was true and really caused them to be like that, I would have killed my kids and ate them!!!! I believe with all my heart that my kids love me and have forgiven me if I did anything bad to them when they were growing up. I pray that they have. At least I feel as though they love me when they all come to my house for Christmas, Thanksgiving and other special occasions every year. They still eat a lot when they come home too!!!! But I love them all with all my heart. I still hug every one of them and I still tell them that I love them even though they are grown and have kids of their own.

I worked hard during my teens and after a failed marriage, I joined the Marine Corps. I had always dreamed of being a Highway Patrol or a Marine. I joined the Marines with every intention of making it a career and retiring from there. When my enlistment was up, I went to reenlist for another six years. The career officer told me that I would definitely go back to Viet Nam two more times during a six year reenlistment and possibly three times. That ended my military career. If they had let us fight that war the way we should have and try to win it, I would have gone back in a heartbeat, but not the way they made us fight it.

My son followed in my footsteps, sort of. He made me the proudest I have ever been when he joined the Marine Corps. I thought the day I graduated from Marine Corps Boot Camp was the proudest I could ever be, but it wasn't. My proudest moment was the day my wife and I flew to San Diego and attended his graduation.

I had finally put most of the ghosts to rest in my mind. Then my son was sent to Kuwait during the war with Iraq. With all the television coverage, that first night when all the fighting broke out we were watching intently. Just knowing he was over there, and in harm's way, my wife and I just looked at each other and I said; "It has started". I may have been more scared at that moment than any time I was in Viet Nam.

It has been thirty years ago today since I left the United States bound for the Republic of Viet Nam. The only reason I am attempting to write about these things now after all these years is that I read about other Marines writing about their experiences that were there when I was. Some of them say that it helped them cope with the memories and nightmares they still have after thirty years when they talk or write about their experiences over there. I haven't talked much about any of the things that happened to me over there for many, many years. My wife, Charlotte finally coaxed me into talking a little about some of the things that happened to me. She has a way of getting me to do a lot of things. Other than that, I have never revealed anything to anyone. She is the reason for this book.

Some of the numbers I mention, or the dates may not be exact because after thirty years of blocking it out, not talking about it and trying to forget it all, makes some things pretty vague. Only *God* and time has helped heal my mind (to a point), but at night, when things are still and quiet, the faces of my best friends who were like my own brothers, that died in that "God-forsaken place" still haunt me. I can't hold back the tears sometimes late at night when the memories creep back into my mind, or I wake up sweating and shaking from the nightmares. Not even time will erase their memories.

I carried a "Kodak Instamatic" camera with me in a plastic bag and took a lot of pictures when I could over there. I have only looked at them two or three times in these thirty years. I hate movies about Viet Nam and the feelings they awaken inside of me. I still can't stand to be around any type of fireworks, because all sudden, unexpected noises unnerve me, but I have gotten a lot better. Time heals a lot of things.

I have never, in any way, felt guilt or shame for fighting in the Viet Nam war. On the contrary, I am fiercely proud of it. I am very proud to have served and fought for my country. What I do feel is disgust, disappointment and repulsion. I want to puke every time I hear a politician praising the Viet Nam Veterans in order to further their political career, especially after the way we were treated when we arrived back home. One in particular is your present President, Bill Clinton. This man was a draft dodger and protestor. He later spat in the face of our entire judicial system and got away with it. Those of you who voted for him gave him the power to send young patriotic Americans to fight and die for their country. This is the same war and the same Veterans that this man protested and refused to serve in.

Some of the things I am going to write about are pretty graphic and may seem cruel and inhumane, but unless you were there and went through it, you could never, ever understand neither the way we felt nor what went through our minds for thirteen long months. I survived Viet Nam and returned home only by the "Grace Of God". I don't know why He allowed me to live through that "thirteen months of HELL" but He did. It was hard for me to understand for a long time why so many good men didn't make it back home.

I was wounded three times and received two Purple Hearts during those thirteen months. I refused the third one, because if a Marine gets wounded three times in one tour of duty, he must be taken out of that war zone. I guess they figure that if you are lucky enough to still be alive after getting wounded three times, you deserve to be sent out of harm's way. When I was wounded the third time, I wasn't ready to leave that place. It may sound crazy, but by then I had a lot of "getting even" to do. The scales were far from being balanced in my mind. They had killed a lot of my friends, but when they killed L/Cpl Dave West, from Dallas Texas, who was closer than a brother to me, I went a little bit crazy. I lost sight of reality, all fear, all the common sense and better judgment I ever possessed. I just wanted to kill as many of those bastards as I could until they killed me. I came as close to losing my mind, as I ever will, because of this and one other significant terrible tragedy. The other thing was the first time I killed a human being. We knew, without a doubt that we were killing them when we were firing a mortar into a group of enemy soldiers or shooting a rifle at them during an ambush. That is different from when you have to kill them up close and in a "one-on-one" situation. When you kill them while looking into their eyes or when they are just a few feet away and you shoot them, there is no doubt who it was that killed them.

We were reacting instead of acting as we were trained to do. Then after it's over and your nerves get back inside your body, and you have time to think, that is when you do your best to pull yourself back together. That is when you cry, puke your guts out or lose your mind a little more each time. But you don't quit, and you don't lose your mind completely, because if you do you will die and you will get a lot of good Marines killed too. With each time and each harrowing experience, it got a little easier to deal with.

13

You finally just accept whatever is headed your way.

The Purple Hearts and the wounds I received, don't affect me much since they have healed, but the mental scars embedded in my mind will never heal. *ANYWAY*—here are just a few of the very many things that happened to me that I could recall during *"MY TOUR OF DUTY"*.

ᴐᴐᴐ

We left California fully trained and well prepared for the next thirteen months we were about to spend in the Republic of South Viet Nam. *"NOT"*!!!!! All of the training on earth could not come close to preparing me for what I was about to experience. Granted all that training and inner strength was a major factor in helping me survive, but nothing on God's green earth could prepare me for what was coming. Maybe the way I grew up with all the hard work, the beatings and verbal abuse made me a good marine. I was mature beyond my years compared to the other kids in my unit. I knew early in my life that nobody would ever beat me or abuse my family or me again and live to tell about it. I have to take exception to that statement when I mention my DI (drill instructor) in boot camp. I thought I had entered the "Gates of Hell" when I arrived at boot camp. Of all the screaming and name-calling I couldn't believe it. They started screaming and barking orders the instant we arrived and kept it up for sixteen long weeks! We were ordered to stand in line and stare at the back of the man's head in front of us. I glanced out of the corner of my eye and saw the guy next to me turning his head and looking around. Just then a DI hit him in the face with his fist and knocked him unconscious. They ordered us to step over him and enter a building where they "sheered" us like sheep. They used clippers without an attachment and cut our hair about one sixteenth of an inch long. The guys who had long hair got the roughest treatment. Those barbers dug the clippers into our scalps so much; some of them left the chair with blood running down all sides of their heads. That was only the beginning.

I have made the statement that I "might" rather spend another tour in Viet Nam than go through Marine Corps boot camp again!!! Not really, but it was quiet an experience. The DI makes you think he is going to kill you and eat you. They tear you down completely, mentally then build you back up the way they want you. They teach you to survive in any situation, and that is a good thing, but I still question some of their tactics.

One time in particular, a guy received a letter from home, which is okay, but he tried to read it after taps (when the lights go out) with a flashlight beneath his blanket. The DI caught him and made him burn the five-page letter in his naked hands and then eat every morsel of the ashes. He made him do pushups until he almost passed out and then crawl to the head (bathroom) with the DI standing on his back, as he held on to the foot of our racks. After they got inside the head, the DI put a metal mop bucket over the guy's head and beat it with a mop handle. I think he damaged his eardrums, because he left our unit, and I think they gave that DI an "undesirable" discharge. This DI is the one who told us numerous times that he knew that none of us would make it home from Viet Nam alive and that when they sent our bodies home, he would "Piss on our caskets." Well, that really improved our frames of mind.

Another time when we were having a weapons inspection, a guy dropped his rifle. He was made to do pushups and other PT until he could do no more, and then dig a hole in the sand. The hole had to be 6x6x6. That meant six feet deep, six feet long, and six feet wide. He had to sleep inside that hole with his rifle all that night, then get up at four a.m. and bury his rifle in that hole. He had to run the fourteen miles before morning chow with us, which we ran every morning in full combat gear. Then he had to run the obstacle course, do hours of PT, then go dig up his rifle and clean it. He had to sleep with his rifle for the next four weeks, and carry it everywhere he went.

We were made to run at full speed and step on top of some

telephone poles that were cut off at different heights and spaced a long step apart. The tops of the first ones were about three feet high and the last ones were about twelve feet up in the air. We did this is in full combat gear and while carrying a thirteen-pound rifle. As we reached the highest poles, we had "to sling" our rifles and jump about fifteen feet and grab hold of some large ropes suspended from a tall tower. We had to climb these ropes to the top and then climb down the other side. One guy made it half way up the rope and could not go any higher. He was holding on about twenty feet above the ground when the DI took hold of the rope at the bottom and began shaking it. He shook the guy loose and he fell to the ground. The weight of all his combat gear (about 65 pounds) and his rifle caused him to break both legs and his pelvis.

Boot Camp was a living hell in itself, but I guess there was a reason for it all. It taught you discipline, to follow orders and to react without thinking, because if you take time to think, in a combat situation, it may cost you your life. I was in pretty good shape when I entered boot camp. I had worked hard all my life and played all sorts of sports in High School. At least I thought I was in good shape. I gained about twenty-five pounds of solid muscle and felt better than I had in my whole life. We didn't like a lot of the things they fed us, but every morsel was good for you. It was the right kinds of food to build a body like they wanted us to have. I came out of boot camp believing that I could "whip the world" and that I was "invincible." You could take all the food you wanted, but you had better eat all you take. Once, I had a large "gricell" in a piece of meat we had. I tried to chew it, but couldn't and it was too big to swallow. I put it into my empty milk carton while holding it underneath the table. I thought there was no way anyone saw me do it. "Wrong"!! When I placed my tray on the counter, my DI made me tear open the milk carton. I had to stand in front of the platoon and eat that gricell and swallow it, then eat most of the carton my milk came in!!!! But it didn't kill

16

me, and I never did anything like that again.

I don't guess it ruined my reputation with the DI, because I was appointed squad leader soon after that.

I was the only squad leader who lasted the entire time. The other three were "demoted" for one reason or another. I knew I didn't want the treatment they received, so I did my best. I had the best squad in our platoon. The recruit who scored the highest on the academic, and the physical tests was awarded a set of Dress Blues. They are the best dress uniform of all branches. Anyone else, who wanted, could buy a set of them. There were several guys in our unit who bought them. I could not afford to buy a set because the total cost was $92.50! I was promoted to PFC upon graduation, which was an honor, because out of the entire unit, only six of us were promoted to PFC when we graduated from boot camp.

Graduation was a wonderful day. Every recruit who graduated in our unit had their families there except three of us. I had no one who came and two guys from the East coast. We acted as if it didn't bother us, but it would have been great to have someone there when we graduated. We left the celebration area and went to the Base Exchange. We walked around the base and just looked at it. That was the first time since we arrived that we were allowed to walk around unsupervised. We even drank a coke, something we were forbidden to do for sixteen weeks.

We flew from El Toro California, which is a Marine Air Wing Training Base. We flew from there to Hawaii. When we heard we were landing in Hawaii, we were all excited. HA!! We landed just long enough to refuel. I can say I have been to Hawaii though, because we stood in formation outside the plane for about thirty minutes. We flew from there to Okinawa where we were to store our sea bags. These sea bags contained all our dress uniforms, shoes and any personal items from home, such as letters with addresses on them, pictures of family etc. We were ordered not to take anything with us for security reasons, in case we were captured and became POW's. We didn't know at the time that the majority of us would never return to this place alive to reclaim our belongings. In fact, I found out after I returned to the states that, out of the three hundred and eleven of us that left our gear in that huge warehouse in Okinawa, only seventy-eight of us survived and returned to claim our gear.

∂∂∂∟

This is the middle of January 2009. I stopped writing on this for a little over eleven more years. I will finish it now, if I can, because I want my children and family to know about this part of my life.

∂∂∂∟

The first morning after we arrived in Okinawa, we went through the normal military routine of "hurry up and wait". We got malaria shots along with a lot more shots of some kind and a last minute physical, which meant nothing. If you were breathing and could walk, you were going on to Viet Nam. Everyone passed. When we landed in Okinawa, I had a bad case of strip throat. I had 103 degree fever, but I didn't tell anyone and avoided the doctors enough to keep them from finding out. I was afraid they would hold me back and the rest of the guys I had trained with and learned to trust would be sent on without me. I joined the Marine Corps to make it a career and fight for my country. I was anxious to get to the war that I had been trained for!!!!

We were restricted to the base while we were in Okinawa because they didn't want us to go AWOL or wind up with VD. The first night there, most of our guys found out from the ones stationed there, that there was a hole in the fence, so they all went out on the town. I would have surely been among them had I not been so sick. The next morning we were issued jungle fatigues, jungle boots, mosquito repellent and all the "essentials" we needed to "do battle" in the jungles of Viet Nam!!!

On the third morning, we got more shots and left Okinawa and flew to the Danang air base. Danang is located about midway of the country, and was controlled by the U.S. Military. It had a makeshift landing strip that they had carved out of the heavy undergrowth of the jungles, just outside the city of Danang. During the flight, all of us were somber and exceptionally quiet with anticipation. I thought of home, my family and wondered, "What had I done"? I don't know about the others, but I tried to envision what lay ahead of me for the next thirteen long months, not knowing at the time, that this was virtually impossible to do. I tried to sleep but couldn't. I tried to pray, but didn't really know how. I felt like I should be scared, but didn't know of what. All I knew was, I was lonely, I missed my family, and I really didn't want to go where I was going and for that matter, I didn't really know why I was going!!!!

When the plane started descending to land on the Danang airstrip, the voice on the intercom started barking out instructions and directions for what they wanted us to do upon touchdown. Whoever was making this announcement sounded awfully excited. As soon as we landed and the plane came to a stop, they rushed us off the plane. There was a whole lot of yelling and in an instant I realized what all the excitement was. Marines were running every which way. Jeeps were driving every direction and going way too fast. Large trucks passed by loaded with black plastic looking bags. These bags were all filled with the bodies of the marines that were killed by the first barrage of mortars and rockets that came in as they all slept in the early morning, before sunrise, and before we arrived.

Several of the plywood staging barracks was still burning, and the whole base was in an uproar. They were still placing bodies in the bags I later learned were appropriately named "body bags". After a long while, things calmed down some and we were sent to the headquarters shack to receive our orders and be assigned to the units we would serve with for our thirteen months tour of duty. We were assigned to units according to the casualty lists. Whichever unit had sustained the highest death loss would get the most of us. We would be the first replacements that Delta Company, 1st Battalion, 26th Marines would receive since leaving the States three months earlier than we did. They were in dire need of replacements because they had seen some "bad shit". They had had more Marines killed and wounded than any military unit in Viet Nam including the Army, when we arrived.

They left the states as a Battalion. A Division consists of four Battalions, a Battalion consists of four Regiments, a Regiment consists of four Companies, a Company consists of four Platoons, a Platoon consists of four squads, and a squad consists of from twelve to sixteen men. Each Company of "grunts" (riflemen) had units attached to them called "cru serve weapons". These weapons consisted of machine guns, mortars, flamethrowers and demolitions.

I got acquainted with a young, baby faced marine on the plane that was in a different training unit in boot camp but the same Company. His name was J.D. and he was from Colorado. He was seventeen years old and turned eighteen on the way over there. Somehow, he looked a lot younger to me. I was twenty-one and looked and felt like an old man compared to these kids on that plane. We both got assigned to "D" Co. 1/26 which was Delta Company, First Battalion, twenty-sixth Marine Regiment. We would be in the First Marine Division, but under the operational control of the Third Marine Division. Delta Company was stationed on HILL 55, which was approximately thirteen miles through the jungle South of Danang where we landed. We were to spend the night here at the Danang airstrip, get weapons and ammunition issued the next morning and then accompany a resupply convoy delivering "C-Rats", water and ammo to them on Hill 55.

We were assigned to a sand bag detail for the rest of the day. We must have filled a million sandbags to rebuild and re-enforce the foxholes and fortify the positions destroyed by the mortars and rockets the night before. Finally, as nighttime approached, we ate some chow, which consisted of a can of cold c-rations. Then we went to one of the plywood barracks that had survived the attack and had cots set up in them for us to sleep on (if you could sleep).

We settled in and finally relaxed a little and talked about home and our families for a while. I lay awake staring into the "nothingness" for a long while after the talking stopped, and sometime much later, drifted off to sleep. I could hear every tiny sound and every movement brought me wide awake and alert, but I finally went sound asleep. About four-thirty a.m. I awoke to the sound that I had dreaded to hear for real for the first time, and it chilled my blood, "INCOMING"!!!!! Several Marines were yelling incoming as loud as they could. I sat up, grabbed my boots and put them on in record time in total darkness. I told J.D. *"let's get the hell out of this building"*! We ran outside to try to find a bunker or a foxhole to get inside of. By then, the mortar rounds and rockets were exploding all around us and all over the base. Those damn gooks had done their homework because they had zeroed in on us pretty good.

Someone, either a gook or our men fired an illumination round into the cold black sky, and we could see where we were going, even though we really didn't know where we wanted to go. After we got a safe distance away from the plywood buildings, we stumbled upon a hole someone had dug, so we jumped inside. The explosions were so close they were deafening and the concussion from them made my chest feel like it would explode. The shrapnel from the mortars made a strange "whizzing" sound as it came over our heads. The shrapnel literally shredded the plywood barracks we had just come from, and caused them to catch on fire.

I heard someone running toward the hole we were in. I raised up just enough to see who it was and a Marine yelled to us that the gooks had broken through the perimeter. If I had never felt it before, I discovered the true meaning of the word "FEAR" at that moment. I looked at J.D. and said; "We have to find a weapon"!!! They were supposed to issue our weapons when we arrived, but with all the damage and commotion, they told us they would issue them the next morning since we were in a "secure" location. There were people running every direction and all of them firing weapons. The barrage of mortars let up for a moment and I told J.D. to "Get up and follow me". I decided that if I was going to die my first night in Viet Nam, I was going to die fighting and not lying in a hole without a weapon.

We ran in a "zig-zag" pattern as we were trained to do, to the other holes until we found one that had received a direct hit with an enemy mortar round. There were three dead marines in and beside it. I jumped inside the hole with them and found two M-14 rifles and a 45-caliber pistol. I took off their cartridge belts, which contained their ammo and told J.D. to help me. We rolled their bodies out of the hole and sat there staring out over them into the pitch black darkness of the night. The attack didn't last very long. After the shooting stopped, we sat there back-to-back in that cold damp hole in the ground, the rest of the night, staring out over those dead marines. We were praying for the sunrise that a lot of these guys would never see.

Finally, dawn came. Everything was blown all to hell, and there were dead and wounded lying everywhere. Some were the gooks that broke through the perimeter that we killed, but most of the dead were marines killed by the mortars and rockets that rained down on us. Intelligence reported that only a small band of VC hit us after the mortar barrage. I guess they must have known they couldn't overrun us and kill us all. They like to hit and run and cause as many casualties as possible. They remind you of a filthy fucking cowardly rat. After the sun came up, we took a body count and we had killed thirteen gooks, but there were twenty-nine marines dead and I can't recall how many wounded.

J.D. and I walked around in disbelief. There were two marines standing beside a foxhole, smoking and talking. They were both wearing "bush hats" and looked really "grungy". As we approached them we could see that they were looking down at a wounded gook inside the foxhole they were standing beside. His right leg had been almost blown off and he had been shot through the stomach. He was mumbling something in Vietnamese. One of the marines standing by the foxhole, calmly and methodically blew the gook's head off with his M-14!!! J.D. and I were both in total shock. I said to him, *"God damn man, I can't believe you did that"*!! The marine said, "You will learn to believe it". And muttered as he walked off, *"That mother-fucker won't kill any more marines."*

I was pretty knowledgeable and I knew about life and death. I grew up on a farm in the Texas Panhandle. I had seen animals give birth, and die. I even had to shoot my own horse when I was ten years old, because he developed "fist aloe", which is a type of cancer that horses develop predominately, in their "withers". I didn't want to kill him, but my dad made me lead him down into the pasture and shoot him. I stayed there with him until way after dark and then walked back to the house. I had hunted and killed wild game all my life. We did our own slaughtering of beef and hogs, so death was nothing new to me. But you throw a country boy like me in the middle of shit like this, and watch a guy kill another human being without any remorse or without batting an eye, and things get a little crazy in a hurry. These were people too. Real human beings just like us, or so I thought at the time. I didn't think I would or could ever in a lifetime feel the way that marine did. I would learn in a short time what he felt and what he meant about my feelings would change.

After we helped carry all the bodies to a collection point, to be placed inside the body bags, put out some fires, and help treat some of the wounded, we turned in the weapons I had taken from the dead marines the night before. We went to the supply shack and checked out an M-14, ammo pouches, canteens, cartridge belts, ponchos, nap sacks and mosquito repellent. We were all issued small bottles of iodine. Ten drops of iodine would supposedly kill all the malaria bacteria germs in one canteen of water. It turned the water a really ugly shade of orange and tasted like crap, but at least it kept us from contracting malaria. Of course after a while, some of the "slackers" left the iodine out of their water so that maybe they would get sick and be sent home.

They gave us all the magazines we wanted and more ammo than I thought I would ever need. Then we reported to the convoy bound for Hill 55, and Delta 1/26. This was the unit and the marines I would spend the next thirteen long, lonely, hazardous months with. We climbed into the backs of the trucks along with all the other supplies headed for Hill 55, and settled in for the long bumpy thirteen-mile trip.

The dirt road leading to Hill 55 wound through the heavy jungles in places, but the road was open in places. It wound through the rice paddies and hills and it was really crooked. Most of the way, it was awful dusty, because the monsoon rains had not set in yet. It was dank and musty smelling when we passed over the road that was covered with the canopy of the heavy trees that overlapped the road forming a sort of tunnel. The lead trucks stirred up a thick stifling cloud of dust as fine as flour. We could barely breathe riding in the back of our truck and couldn't see a thing at times. Sometime, the driver of our truck was forced to drop back in the convoy to avoid the heavy dust and to be able to see where he was driving. It seemed dangerously too far from the truck ahead of us, because the gooks liked to hit us at our weakest point and time.

I guess this road was pretty secure, at least as secure as it could be. "Huey Helicopters" flew over pretty often and we met a couple of Platoon size-patrols and another patrol with a mine sweeping crew. They checked the road every morning to be sure that "Charlie" had not set any land mines or booby traps the night before. I found out later that they almost always found some of both every morning. The Viet Cong controlled the nights and the monsoon seasons.

We reached Hill 55 without incident, and as the rough riding trucks lumbered along and the motors labored to climb the steep winding road to the top of the hill, I couldn't help but think to myself, "What a beautiful, majestic scene in the valley below the hill". It would have made a beautiful painting with the rich green rice paddies submerged in water, and the dark green foliage of the jungles nearby and the thin line of the crooked dusty road winding through them. It was hard for me to imagine that there was death lurking behind every rice paddy dike and banana tree in this jungle, for all who entered there.

We unloaded our sea bags full of new combat gear and slung them over our shoulders and headed to the top of the hill where the headquarters tent was set up. It was on the very top of the hill. The hill had an outer perimeter with "consentina wire" (tangled barbed wire) encircling it. This sharp barbed wire was unrolled all the way around the top of the hill to prevent the gooks from rushing us in force. At least when they attacked, the wire would slow them down enough that we might kill enough of them to even the odds a little. Just inside the wire, there were bunkers dug into the sides of the hill with sandbags piled up in front to provide protection from sniper fire and shrapnel from hand grenades or mortar rounds exploding around the bunker. They built a bunker that held riflemen, then one with machine gunners, then one with 60 MM Mortars, in that order all the way around the hill. This was called our "outer perimeter".

The Company Commander gave us a short orientation of how things were going, what to expect and what our responsibilities would be. He didn't paint a very bright picture, because as I mentioned, this Company had been through hell. He was a young Captain (maybe twenty three years old), and explained that they had just returned from an amphibious landing into the DMZ (Demilitarized Zone), "NO MAN'S LAND", and that he had received word that we might make another similar assault. There weren't supposed to be any troops inside the DMZ, not theirs not ours. We are probably the only nation in the world who follows the rules during wartime. Evidently the North Vietnamese had been inside the DMZ a long time, because they had permanent cement bunkers, machine gun positions built and booby traps set up everywhere. There had been three companies involved in the assault, but Delta Company was the spearhead of the operation and therefore, suffered the most casualties. J.D. and I were replacements for the ones who got killed and wounded.

The C.O. sent us to the Platoon Commander of the third platoon. He was even younger than the Company Commander! He was a punk kid that was maybe nineteen years old. He looked like he should have still been in High School, but he had been through O.C.S. (Officers Candidate School) and was a second lieutenant.

My MOS (Military Occupation Specialty) was 0351, which was rocket launchers, flamethrowers and demolitions. I had also been specially trained to disarm all types of landmines and booby-traps that the NVA and VC were known to use. A rocket launcher is a hand held, shoulder fired "rocket launcher". It was an awesome weapon and relatively light and mobile. The gooks hated them, because we traveled along with the infantry on patrols and could do major damage to their ambushes. A flamethrower is two tanks mounted on a backpack and is filled with "Napalm". This stuff is some really bad stuff. It is a liquid, thicker than honey and highly volatile. The flamethrower has an "igniter" on the gun at the end of a hose leading from the tanks. It will shoot the thick, burning liquid a long distance. We used them to force gooks out of the caves and tunnels where they hid to ambush us. They would dive inside these tunnel complexes and disappear unless we burned them out, blew them out or went inside after them. That was a scary, dangerous job too. We also used the flamethrowers to burn off vegetation from the hilltops where we set up and occupied them for any length of time. The military used defoliants to kill the vegetation and heavy jungles. One in particular that they used was called "Agent Orange". Many years later, the U S Government finally admitted that these defoliants caused cancer in multitudes of Viet Nam Vets. They would fly over us and dump these chemicals and they didn't care that they were drenching us with this potent, toxic liquid. They mostly used this stuff down South where the Army was. Up North, where we were, we primarily used the flamethrowers and machetes to clear away the jungles.

With the demolitions as part of my MOS, I was trained to blow things up. We used "C-4" as the main explosive along with some more, but C-4 was the main one. It came in small, square "bricks" about three inches square and a foot long. It was extremely safe to handle. You could throw it down, stomp on it, submerge it in water or even chew it. We would break off small pieces and set it on fire to heat our C-rations with. It made a blue flame and burned really hot. It was safe until you applied an electric charge or a blasting cap. Then it was the most potent explosive we had access to at that time. One stick of C-4 strategically placed beneath a three bedroom house would complete obliterate the house. It would turn it into splinters. We used C-4 to blow the tunnels, knock down huge trees and to blow up large caches of weapons and ammunition we confiscated from the gooks. Most of the weapons and ammo we took from them were Russian and Chinese made. We also took a lot of American made weapons and munitions that the gooks had taken when they over ran an Army stronghold or base camp.

Another explosive we used was "Det Cord" (detonation cord). This stuff was bad too. It was pretty potent by itself, but when we connected it to C-4 it enhanced its destructive power immensely. The thing that made it so bad was that when it was ignited on one end, it blew up simultaneously. That means whether it was twenty feet long or twenty miles long, the entire length of it blew up at the very same instant. It is the same stuff they use today to fell large buildings.

A few days before we left the states, I put in a request to change my MOS. I did a lot of thinking and decided if I had a choice, I had rather go into combat as an 0311. The 0311 MOS is a "grunt" which is a plain old rifleman. I thought I would be a lot better off just carrying a rifle instead of all that other stuff. I got yelled at, chastised and was told in no uncertain terms that the Marine Corps had not wasted all that time, money and training on me to allow me to go to Viet Nam as a grunt. I had finished first in my class during training so they had plans for me to lead and teach others when I got overseas.

Well, I guess the rules were different in a war zone! When we arrived at the third platoon's location on the hill, we met the Platoon Sergeant. He showed us around their position and as we approached a mortar pit, on the South side of the hill overlooking the lush green valley I had observed when we arrived at Hill 55. He asked me, "*PFC Stephens, how much do you know about 60 Millimeter mortars?*" I told him I had seen pictures of one, but that I had never seen one up close and knew nothing about them. He said, "*You are about to get acquainted with them*". As it turned out, when the gooks attacked us at the Danang airstrip, they also hit Hill 55 the night before. The gunner of a 60MM Mortar had been killed during the attack along with six other marines. He explained that there was no one else trained on the mortars, so "I was IT". He said I would have three days to learn everything there was to know about the mortar. A gunner on one of the three mortar teams attached to Delta Company would train me. Hell, I had just spent sixteen long, tedious weeks in basic training trying to learn about rocket launchers, demolitions and flamethrowers and there was a lot I still didn't know about them. How in the world did he expect me to learn all there was to know about a 60 in three days? "But" somehow, I did. We went over the nomenclature and firing procedure what seemed like a thousand times in those three days and nights. If I was going to have to carry this weapon into combat, I wanted to know it inside and out. We had plenty of mortar rounds on the hill, so I got to fire it a lot in those three days. I got to where I could set it up and fire it in my sleep and in record time, which was a must. Being able to set up and fire within seconds of the first shot of an ambush would save a lot of lives, including my own. I hadn't had time to think about the reality of when that first shot is fired, everyone else "hits the deck" and dives for cover. I wouldn't be afforded that luxury. When that first shot rang out, I had to get my team together, grab the bi-pods and sight from my A-Gunner, assemble the gun, set the sight for a certain range and fire the gun. While I was assembling the gun and getting ready to fire, I was telling my ammo humpers to open a certain number of mortar rounds and lay them out so my A-Gunner could drop them down the mortar tube upon my command. After a while and after a few times we were ambushed, this all became second nature.

As I said, there were three mortar teams in Delta Company. Each team consisted of a gunner, an A-gunner and three ammo humpers. A 60 MM mortar round weighs approximately seven pounds including the canister. As the gunner, I would carry the tube and base plate of the gun. My A-gunner would carry the bipods and sight. He would take over as gunner during a fire fight should I get killed, so he had to know the gun as well as I did. The three ammo humpers would carry seven mortar rounds each. They carried them inside their packs, tied on top with a strap and even in the large pockets of their jungle fatigues. The entire mortar assembled weighs forty-seven pounds. The tube and base plate that I carried weighed thirty-two pounds. I carried it over my shoulder with the base plate resting on my pack to relieve some of the weight off my shoulder joint. We had to carry all of these things in addition to our personal weapons, ammo for them and our poncho. We carried C-rations for the duration of the patrol we were on at the time (sometimes four days), and at least four canteens full of water. I carried all of this, along with maps of the area and more things we might need. Altogether, I carried about ninety-six pounds of gear. Hell, I only weighed one hundred and sixty eight pounds myself!!!

Of the three mortar teams attached to Delta Company, one was placed on the East side of the hill, one on the South side and the third on the West side of the hill. The North side of the hill was relatively secure, because the road leading back to Danang was on the North side and there was always activity and patrols going out in that direction. My mortar pit was on the South side of the hill. I shot azimuths and plotted potential targets and estimated ranges to those targets during the daylight. I drove aiming stakes in the sandbags that lined the front of my bunker. At night if there was no immediate action going on, we fired at these preplotted targets. I set the gun so that we would have "interlocking fire" with the other guns. That meant our right and left limits of firing direction would overlap with the guns on each side of us. In doing this, we could cover the entire landscape without any dead spots or blind spots.

Our pit was an open hole about eight feet in diameter and approximately three feet deep. The first night, we rotated watches. Since we were the new guys, J.D. and I would stand the first two watches. The first watch lasted from eight P.M. until midnight. I would stand the first. The second watch was from midnight until four A.M., and the last watch from four until daylight, when everyone woke up and started stirring around. This may have been the second longest night of my life. The first being the night before at the airstrip. When our watch was over, we were supposed to sleep the rest of the night. HA!!! There is no way that anybody on earth fresh from the states, being use to nice clean, warm and safe beds could have slept in this damp dirt hole in the ground. Especially while the sounds of war were echoing through the   night, and what with everything that had happened the night before at the Danang base camp.

I hadn't realized how completely tired, exhausted and drained I really was until I leaned back against the cool damp earth of the bunker. My mind was racing and a tremendous amount of fear and anxiety welled up inside of me as I saw everyone except me, sound asleep. As I looked around, I came to one conclusion, and it was that "My new home wasn't near big enough or deep enough". An eight foot hole that is three feet deep is not nearly adequate enough for five marines, all their worldly possessions, a 60 MM mortar set up ready to fire, ammo and C-Rations. Something had to give.

When my watch was over, I woke J.D. and made sure he was wide awake before I lay down and at least tried to relax and rest for a while. It was no use. It was too crowded inside the hole so I rolled outside the hole and stretched out on the ground next to it. It felt good to stretch out, but the sticks and rocks I was lying on made it impossible to relax. Besides that and the frame of mind I was in, there were the insects! I think there must have been more species of biting insects in the jungles and rice paddies of Viet Nam than anywhere on earth.

Sleeping outside your foxhole was a definite "NO-NO"! The first incoming rocket or mortar round, or a sniper's bullet from the bottom of our hill just a few yards away, could end your career and your life in the blink of an eye. Sometime, much later, I must have dozed off and slept for a while. I guess the exhaustion finally took its toll on me.

At last, dawn came and I awoke to the sounds of marines stirring around on the hill and the night patrols and listening posts coming up the crooked winding trail from the jungle. They gave the predesignated passwords as they passed through the narrow opening in the thick tangled consentina wire encircling the hilltop. There were night ambushes and listening posts set up each night, a few hundred meters from our hill to prevent the gooks from sneaking up on us or initiating a large scale assault. I thought to myself as they slowly snaked up the hill that I really wouldn't like to be out there all night with just a few marines. They are out there alone, exposed and vulnerable, but really a necessity.

As the sun rose and other patrols left the hill to travel a predesignated route through an area of the jungle, we ate "breakfast."

My first breakfast in Viet Nam was a cold can of "Ham and MFers" (as they were called). These were large green lima beans with tiny chunks of ham and all of it floating in a thick soupy layer of cold grease!! This was the year of 1966 and the C-Rations we were issued were canned in 1947!!! We knew this was true, because the dates were stamped on the cases and on the cans of C-Rats. We had to throw some of them away because the liquid was seeping out at the rusted seams in the cans. We ate the ones that weren't leaking. After we ate what we could stand, a gunner from another gun team came to our pit. We checked the location of the patrols and did some more practice firing in the opposite direction with my "new weapon".

The mortar has four parts, the tube, the base plate, the sight and the bipods. The tube, where the mortar round is dropped in, is about four inches in diameter and thirty inches long. There is a firing pen and a trigger mechanism at the base of the tube. It snaps into the base plate, which is about fourteen inches square with spikes protruding from the bottom of each corner. These spikes prevent the gun from jumping around during a fire mission. The bi-pods are two adjustable folding legs with two cranks. One is for elevation and one for "windage" to move the tube from side to side. The sight has a peephole to align with the target and two leveling bubbles. One bubble is for elevation and one for the side-to-side leveling. There is a chart inside each case of mortar rounds which tells you what charge to use for a certain distance and what numbers the sight should be set on to coincide with that charge. Then you just level the bubbles and fire. I had to readjust the cranks and bubbles after each round was fired, due to the tremendous "kick" of the round being fired. If it wasn't set up right, the whole mortar would jump violently and sometimes even fall over.

There are three different types of mortar rounds. There is an HE round which stands for High Explosive. This is the one we used most. There is a WP round which is a White Phosphorous (also called "Willie Peter"). We used it to mark an area to call in air strikes on the enemy. It puts off a huge plume of white smoke that the pilots can see from long distances and can drop their bombs on a pinpointed location. There is an illumination round which we used to light up the night skies during the nights when the gooks attacked us or made an attempt to over run our positions. It puts off a brilliant light rated at about five million candlepower.

The 60 MM Mortar is an amazingly accurate weapon up to four thousand meters and can wreak havoc on the enemy when fired accurately. Dry ammo is a must with this weapon. If you fire damp or wet ammo, this weapon is notorious for "short rounds". That means when you set the gun up to fire at a distance of two thousand meters, it might only go about twenty meters and then explode! When that happens, that round could explode inside your own perimeter and kill or wound your own troops. They were so bad about having short rounds that we were ordered to never fire over the heads of our own troops unless it was an extreme emergency.

As I said, I learned the 60 well and within a few days, I was taking my gun team on patrols with the riflemen and "humping" (carrying) the mortar. The grunts carried extra mortar rounds for us too. Most of them never complained, because when we walked into an ambush and were severely outnumbered, they were awfully glad we had plenty of ammo. A good mortar team can break up an ambush pretty fast when we start blowing the hell out of our attackers.

One day we were on patrol on our way to a village to check out reports of suspected VC activity. When we approached the village, we were attacked from the grass "hooches" (huts) in the village and from the tree line around the village with small arms fire and RPG's (rifle propelled grenades). A sniper shot my A-gunner in the throat and killed him with the first volley. I yelled for my ammo humpers to break out the ammo from their canisters. I didn't wait for a fire mission order. I told one of my ammo humpers to get the sight from the dead A-gunners pack. When he raised up to get the sight the sniper killed him instantly! By now, things were pretty haywire. Everyone was returning fire toward the village and my platoon leader was yelling for me to get some rounds fired into that village. I slammed the base plate into the mud to "seat" it (so it wouldn't jump around). I held the tube with my hands without the bi-pods or sight; at an angle toward the village that I thought was right and told one of the men I had left, to drop a round into the tube. It exploded about thirty meters short and off to the left a little of the first hooch. I adjusted the angle and told him to start dropping rounds in the tube as fast as he could. The second round hit on the roof of the grass hooch and it disintegrated!! All the other rounds exploded inside the small village, causing extensive damage and casualties. The firing from the village stopped. We entered the village and as we suspected, it was deserted. The gooks had pulled a hasty retreat and all the villagers or "civilians" were gone too. They always seemed to disappear when the VC planned to ambush us from their villages. Thinking back now, I guess the real civilians had no choice. The VC would have killed them too if they hadn't left. We found twelve dead VC and three wounded too bad to evacuate with their buddies. My mortar had done a job on them.

We called in medi-vac helicopters and loaded our dead and wounded to be air lifted out. I had two dead men out of the five of us. There was a machine gunner wounded really badly and there were four dead grunts. Things settled down a little and one of my men said, "Tony, look at your hands"!! I looked at my hands and they were both solid, clear blisters. I hadn't even noticed that the tube had gotten extremely hot and just roasted my hands. After I became aware of the burns, I realized it hurt like hell! The platoon sergeant told me to get on board the medi-vac chopper and fly back to the hill, but I wouldn't. I pushed my hands down into the cool wet mud of the rice paddy and one of my men wrapped them with bandages. I stayed with the patrol until we returned to our hill. I decided right then something had to change if I was going to fire this thing without the bi-pods. When we got back to the hill, I cut the top and bottom out of two canteen pouches. They are made of really heavy canvas and lined with heavy wool. They were just the right size to slide down over the mortar tube. They worked great.

Days turned into weeks and the fear of dying every second of every minute of every day and night subsided a little and I guess I just accepted the fact that if I was going to die here, then "so be it"! A man can go completely insane and lose his mind living in constant fear after a certain amount of time. I was resolved to the fact that a lot of marines had lived through this hellhole and maybe, just maybe I could too.

After my A-gunner got killed, I asked the CO whether or not J.D. could join my team and he agreed to let him if I would train him. His MOS had been the same as mine when we left the states. From that day forth, for the rest of my tour, J.D. was with me.

The way I fired the mortar during the ambush I talked about was referred to as "Kentucky Windage". I got so good using Kentucky wind age with my mortar that I wouldn't even take the bi-pods or sight on patrols. I got to where I could out shoot the other mortar teams that were using their sights and bi-pods because I didn't have to assemble and level the gun before, and during the firing. I would just slam the base plate into the ground hold the tube with my "makeshift potholders" that I devised and call for mortar rounds. We had a lot of rounds that had been rained on or the canisters were damaged. The CO told us to take it outside the perimeter and "blow it" with C-4. Before we exploded it, we asked the Captain for permission to shoot some of it for practice.

We had a sort of contest to see which gun team could set up the fastest and fire the most accurate. One time in particular, the

Gunnery Sergeant yelled *"Fire Mission"*!! We all scrambled to our guns as he said *"Target; large clearing, fifteen hundred meters south"*! There was a huge dead tree in the middle of the clearing and I jokingly asked the Gunny if he wanted me to hit that tree? He said, *"Stephens, quit being a wise-ass"*. *"You will be lucky to even hit the clearing without using a sight"*. I leaned the tube toward the clearing at an angle I thought was right and fired my mortar. I couldn't believe my eyes. The first round I fired hit that tree and blew it into a thousand pieces! Gunny Teague just shook his head and looked at the Captain and said, *"I told you he was good"*.

From that day forward, if ever there was a patrol pinned down or someone needed deadly accurate mortar support, close in to their position, they called for my gun team. After I had been in country for about four months, I was promoted to Corporal and assigned as "section leader" of all three-mortar teams. But I never completely relinquished my role as a gunner on my mortar. I had learned to love it and I was really good at it. A promotion should be something to be proud of, especially a combat promotion, but now I would be responsible for the lives of fifteen men instead of just the five in my team. I would be responsible for assigning them watches, duties on the hill and for sending them out on patrols with the grunts. Patrols that I knew without a doubt, that some of them would never return from. I would also have to inspect their mortars, weapons and mortar pits.

Keeping your weapons clean, whatever kind you carried, was the single most important task you would ever have. It was your life. If a weapon didn't function properly, your chances of survival diminished drastically and rapidly. When headquarters called for three or four men to go on work details, patrols or to ride shotgun on resupply convoys I had to decide who would be sent and do my best to be fair about it. I had the distinction of listening to all their personal problems too. They looked up to me and came to me with all their woes.

Weeks turned into months and I was still alive!!! I got to thinking *"maybe, just maybe I might make it through this shit alive"*!!! We became the "old salts", the "short timers", and the ones with a measurable amount of time "in country". We had lost so many men that it was time for us to receive more replacements. These new replacements considered us lucky, because we had a lot less time than they did before we could leave this terrible place and go home. As some of the marines within the Company started rotating back to the States, and new replacements took their places, I remember thinking, *"Surely, I was not as green or scared looking as these kids were"*!! But I probably was and looked just as bad to the ones who had been there for ten long months or so.

Anyway, now we were the short timers counting the days and marking them off on our calendars one-by-one as each day we survived became more precious than the day before. And believe me, it was a miracle to survive from one day to the next. We all knew that one split second of becoming too passive or getting lax could end it all. Of course, you didn't even qualify as a short timer until you made it "over the hump", which meant that you had been in country for six months, two weeks and one day. That equaled exactly one day past the half way point of the thirteen months we were destined to stay in this God-forsaken place "if" we lived that long.

As I have mentioned, Delta 1/26 occupied Hill 55 and was a very mobile unit. At one time we were the most mobile unit in Viet Nam. We went to the "hot spots" which meant where the heaviest fighting was from North of Danang, South almost to Saigon. Our job was to stay on constant alert and be ready to move out at a moment's notice, day or night. We answered any and all distress calls immediately when we received them. Sometimes they would load us into helicopters and sometimes we would do a force march to the action. It all depended on how far away the fighting was.

Alpha and Bravo Companies were located east and a little south of Hill 55 about four thousand meters. The road that we

37

took from Danang to Hill 55 continued on past our hill, across a wide stream and on to where A and B companies were located. The road ran along the outskirts of an area we called "Death Valley". It was named Death Valley because there had been such a tremendous number of marines killed there. There was about thirty square miles of heavy jungle and it was literally infested with VC. We lost men every time we patrolled that area. Charlie Company's headquarters was located Southwest of us about two thousand meters. We had to take their supplies, water and ammo to them by chopper because there were no roads leading to their position, only jungle and rice paddies.

We were "standing down" after a four-day operation, cleaning weapons and getting resupplied when Charlie Company called us. We had just arrived back on our hill and were "licking our wounds". They said they were in a "world of shit", and were in immediate danger of being over run by at least a Battalion size force of NVA (North Vietnamese Army). We thought the report was odd, because we seldom ever encountered the NVA in this area, mostly just VC (Viet Cong). They said they had suffered heavy casualties, and that "sappers" had penetrated their perimeter (these were suicidal little bastards). They ran right at a large group of us or dove inside the command bunker with a satchel of explosives. They knew we would kill them anyway, so they just blew themselves up for any chance of killing us. We were still exhausted and nowhere near ready for another battle like this, but we were Charlie Company's only hope, so we saddled up with fresh ammo, and other supplies and boarded the choppers in less than twenty minutes after the desperate call for help came.

The choppers dropped us in a clearing about five hundred meters from Charlie Company's position. Our CO sent the first and second platoons around to the North of their position. He sent the fourth platoon around to the South. I sent one mortar team with the first platoon and one with the fourth platoon. I took the other team with third platoon and we advanced straight ahead toward the worst of the fighting and toward the center of Charlie Company's location. When we got about two hundred meters from the worst of the fighting, the CO told me to "*get some mortar rounds in the air*". I gathered all the rounds we had brought with us and had my men open all of them and lay them out next to my gun. I knew that once we started firing and the NVA located our position, we would need all of them. I fired ten well-placed rounds as fast as I could and as close in to Charlie Company's perimeter as possible without hitting them.

The mortar rounds came as a total shock to the NVA, because they didn't know we were anywhere in the area. The brutal assault on Charlie Company subsided momentarily. This few minutes of hesitation allowed our three other platoons time to circle around and hit the NVA from two directions. That wasn't really such a good thing!!! When our other platoons attacked them from two different sides, they had nowhere to go except in our direction! They were retreating way too fast and right toward us. We only had a platoon and here was what was left of a Battalion of gooks desperately trying to get away. This was the same size force that had just a while earlier, almost over run a whole company of Marines. We had to try and stop them with just a platoon!

Once the NVA got close to our position, the mortar was of no use, because it fires at long ranges in a high arc. We fixed bayonets, used rifles, pistols and everything we had when they reached our location. Remnants of Charlie Company had joined our other three platoons and were right in behind the gooks, but they couldn't get to us because the NVA was between them and us. We killed a lot of NVA that day, but not without sacrifice.

We had a total of sixty-eight men in third platoon counting my five-man mortar team, and a three-man machine gun team, when we responded to Charlie Company's cry for help. When the smoke cleared, we had suffered something awful. The NVA killed sixteen of us and wounded seventeen more. There were only thirty-five of us out of sixty-eight that weren't dead or wounded. That was my first encounter with close up hand-to-hand combat and I prayed that it would be my last, but my prayers weren't answered.

It took us two long hard days to extract our dead and wounded and to get Charlie Company resupplied and settled back in. We had to rebuild their bunkers and string more consentina wire. They had lost so many men before we got to them that our CO left third platoon there to man the vacant positions until they could get some replacements. The four-day operation we had just returned from plus these two days, made six days and nights we had just gone through with little or no sleep and rest. We also had very little time or opportunity to eat.

We boarded the choppers and flew back to Hill 55 with what healthy men we had left and welcomed the opportunity to rest for three whole days without a cry for help. We cleaned our weapons, restocked our ammo and relaxed as best we could. When the action slows or stops for a while, you have time for your mind to think of other things. The reality of what all had just happened sets in and "grips you like a vice". We all prayed to God to let us live through this nightmare, and prayed for the families of those who would never make it home.

Things were relatively quiet for a few days after that, so we had a chance to write letters home, organize what worldly possessions we had, (which wasn't much), and visit with guys from our home states back in the "real world". We had a tendency to get more acquainted with guys from the same state as us. There were six or seven of us from Texas in the third platoon, so we visited when we had time. Even though we lived some six hundred miles apart back home, we felt like we were from the same neighborhood. I became really good friends with a red headed guy from Dallas Texas named Dave West. The DI s in boot camp had warned us to never get too close to any one person over there. He tried to warn us of the consequences of letting that happen, then having to carry your friend's body out of an area after he gets killed.

We were sitting outside my bunker one night, just shooting

the bull when one of the new replacements decided to light a cigarette. Those of us who had been there for a while knew to cup both hands around the lighter and over the end of the cigarette each time you take a puff. It would amaze the average person to know just how far the fire on the end of a cigarette can be seen in the dark of night. Anyway, he lit the cigarette without cupping his hands over it and just then, a sniper somewhere in the edge of the tree line opened fire with an AK-47!! There were sparks flying around us everywhere caused by the bullets hitting rocks. The mayhem only lasted a few seconds because the last thing those snipers wanted was for us to pinpoint his location. Luckily, no one was hit this time, but four of us had dived inside the mortar pit and two more dove behind the bunker. We all laughed after it was over but it could have been and often was, really bad. The machine gun bunker next to my pit open fire on the tree line where he thought he saw a muzzle flash from the sniper's rifle. We went down and checked it out, but couldn't find any bodies. The gooks were sneaky and elusive. The kid who lit the cigarette cupped his hands over the end of them from then on! This was one of the comical things I would write home about.

I wrote letters home every chance I got which wasn't very often. I wrote because I knew my whole family was worried sick about me and I didn't want that. I never told any of them about the bad things that happened or what I was going through, because I knew they could never understand. Unless you were there, you could never understand some of the things that happened. I would just tell them the funny or lighthearted things. The only time I ever wrote home about what really happened was when I got wounded because I was afraid they would hear about it on some news program. I knew they would send my Purple Hearts to my home address, so I wrote home as soon as I could and told them it was only a scratch!

Besides the rats, leeches, malaria, snakes, and biting insects we had to contend with every day, we had a terrible problem with "jungle rot". The medical term or scientific name for it was "immersion foot". It was caused from unsanitary conditions and was an infection similar to athlete's foot, only much, much worse. You could get it anywhere on your body, but it was more prevalent on our feet. Our feet were more susceptible because we waded through the muck and mud every waking moment during the monsoons, and almost every other day on patrols through the rice paddies. The gook civilians fertilized the rice paddies with human waste! Every village collected all the human waste and spread it out over the rice paddies for fertilizer; therefore all of the rice paddies were one big cesspool. We had to be especially careful when we would get cuts from the "Elephant Grass" which always happened. The edges of the leaves on the elephant grass

My mortar, flak jacket and lots of "Elephant Grass". The heat and weight got unbearable at times.

would cut you like a razor. The sores caused by leeches after you removed them were a main concern. Once, I caught two black guys in one of my mortar teams intentionally trying to get jungle rot. They were gutless cowards and I told them if they got the jungle rot, I would make them go on patrol anyway and shoot their "F-ing feet" off and leave them in the jungle to die! They were using a piece of spent brass from a rifle shell to scratch the blood out of a place on their feet. Then they wouldn't report it or let their feet air out until it turned into jungle rot. They did this so they wouldn't have to go on patrol or stand watch. I should have just shot them or court marshaled them when I caught them doing it. Their buddies had done it and got away with it. It only takes a couple of days for an untreated sore to develop into a really bad case of jungle rot. The Corpsman, when they finally reported it recommended that they be put on light duty and not go on patrols. I just figured that I didn't want any sorry SOB like that in the bush with me, or watching my back.

The rest of us took our boots off and let our feet air out every chance we got. Fresh air and clean, dry socks was the best way to ward off the jungle rot, but we seldom if ever had the socks. No matter how hard we tried or how much we aired our feet out, we all got a case of it from time to time, due to the filth and not getting to bathe for days and weeks at a time. After our socks rotted off our feet, we just wore our boots without socks. We never seemed to be able to get more uniforms.

When things seemed too quiet and calm for a few days at a time, we got nervous, and usually with good reason. Our patrols would get longer and more frequent, because we knew the gooks were planning something. Once, aerial recon reported increased VC activity about five thousand meters to the South of our location. First and third platoons were ordered to venture to that location and report any findings back to intelligence. I volunteered to go with them and took two of my mortar teams with us. The third team would stay on the hill for security. This was supposed to be a "recon" patrol. We were to avoid contact with the enemy at all costs. "Not so easy"!

We had traveled just over two thousand meters through the rice paddies and jungle when we came to a road. We had a "boot" second lieutenant fresh from the states who had taken over command of third platoon. He decided it would be much easier and faster to just walk down the road for a while. The rest of us knew this was the wrong thing to do, but he had the rank. We were exposed from all sides and out in the open. We had gone maybe a hundred meters down the road when the man walking point, about ten meters ahead of me, stepped on a land mine. Those things were designed to blow up a jeep or blow the track off a tank. You can imagine what it did to a human body!

His upper torso, from his belt up was all that came down in tact. But I had very little time to think about what had just happened before my eyes. When the mine exploded, the gooks in a well-laid ambush hit us from our left flank. We instinctively jumped behind the elevated road on the opposite side. They had planned for this maneuver, because most of their firepower was positioned in the tree line on our right flank.

They were too close for me to use the mortar. I only carried a .45 caliber pistol as my personal weapon, because I needed both hands free to carry and fire the mortar. I picked up an M-14 rifle from one of the marines who was killed during the first volley, and returned fire toward the tree line. They had us in a bad way. I told my ammo humpers to break out some mortar rounds. I slammed my base plate into the side of the elevated bank of the road and tilted the tube in the direction of the ambush. I told my a-gunner to drop the rounds and I used the manual trigger mechanism to fire them. I was firing the mortar more like a big shoulder fired weapon, but using the road bank as my shoulder. After I had fired six rounds into the tree line, the ambush subsided. They hit us hard and did some damage. We only had eight dead, but we had six more wounded. The gooks knew we never left a marine, neither dead nor wounded, behind. They withdrew and slinked back into the heavy jungle, knowing that we would not chase them. They were sneaky little bastards.

After carrying the eight bodies up on the road and treating the wounded, we picked up what was left of the point man's body that had stepped on the mine. Two guys carried his upper torso and I picked up the boot that hadn't stepped on the mine. *His foot was still inside his boot!!!* The mine had obliterated the foot he stepped on the mine with, and blew his other foot off that I picked up.

After the medi-vac choppers left with the bodies and the wounded, we continued on the patrol. The Lt. knew I had training in land mines and booby traps, so he told me to walk point. I wanted to tell him that I had training disarming them, not finding them!!! But I just took point and said nothing, because someone had to do it. I let my A-Gunner carry my mortar tube and kept the dead marine's rifle I had picked up, and led out.

We left the road after a while and followed a jungle trail through the thick canopy of the jungle and the heavy Elephant Grass. The elephant grass is a lot like the Johnson grass we had back home, only it grew about eight feet tall and a lot tougher than Johnson grass. If the edge of the leaves slid down your face, neck, hands or any exposed skin, it would cut you really bad. We continued down the path for a ways and were approaching a village. We could see the village in the distance so we were on alert and very apprehensive. We knew from past experience that the gooks loved to ambush us or snipers liked to shoot at us from the villages because we always tried to avoid killing any civilians. The gooks didn't care who they killed. They killed a lot of the villagers on purpose.

Since I was on point and the first in line to get shot at, I momentarily forgot my main objective, and that was to check for land mines and booby traps! I had my eyes trained on the village ahead, trying to detect any movement or unusual activity

45

that might reveal the slightest hint of an ambush. I didn't even notice that the trail had suddenly become covered with grass and banana leaves. In an instant too late, I realized that I was walking on the grass and leaves instead of the dirt trail that I had been walking on. With my very next step, the leaves gave way under my feet and down I went. I knew instantly what it was. I had fallen into a "Punji-Pit"!!

The soil in the Southern part of Viet Nam is firm, almost like clay, so the gooks could dig perfectly square holes. They dug them about five feet deep and four feet square, then shave the sides straight up. Being this type of soil, you could step near the edge of the holes and the ground would not cave in under your weight. Your boot could be halfway over the edge of the side and not cave off. At the bottom of these pits, the gooks would sharpen bamboo stalks needle sharp about two feet long and stand them up with the sharp end pointing skyward. Before they put them in the pits, they would soak them in human waste, which is the most concentrated form of germs I know of. If you fall into one of these pits, the "Punji-Stakes" will impale you and stick completely through your body.

When my lead foot stepped on the grass and it gave way, I realized the fix I was in. My back foot was still on solid ground, so I tried to leap forward with it, because I knew these pits usually weren't very wide. I didn't make it. I fell into the pit. Once more (of the many times), God took me by the hand. We hadn't been issued the "M-16" rifles yet so we still had the old trusty M-14 rifles. If I had been carrying an M-16, I would have surely died right then and there. The M-14 is a heavy well-built weapon approximately five feet long, (the pit was four feet wide). The muzzle of the rifle landed on one side of the pit and the stock landed on the other side. Somehow, the rifle came up into my armpits and up against my chest. I was literally hanging, suspended over the stakes of the punji-pit with all my weight on the rifle. The guys right behind me saw my predicament and started toward me. I yelled for them to get down, because ordinarily when we stumbled upon one of these pits, an ambush came along with it.

I felt excruciating pain in my left leg, just below my knee. After no ambush erupted, I yelled for someone to help me, because I knew the rifle would not keep supporting my weight. Two guys ran over and took hold of my arms and helped me out of the pit. The corpsman came and looked at my leg. One of the punji stakes had hit my leg about mid-way up my shinbone, and slid up the bone until it hit my knee bone. Luckily for me, that is when the rifle stopped my fall. I have helped get men out of these pits that fell to the bottom. The stakes entered their bodies in their buttocks or crotch area and penetrated all the way through them and came out through their chests or around their collarbones. It is a hell of a way to die. The corpsman cleaned and doctored my leg then wrapped it with a battle dressing. He wanted to call in a medi-vac chopper, but we were so deep into "death valley" and the jungle was so dense, a chopper couldn't get to us. I continued on down the trail leading the patrol.

When we finally returned to the hill, the Company Commander recommended me for another Purple Heart, but I refused it because that would have been my third one and I was not ready to leave Viet Nam yet. I still had a lot of getting even to do.

When J.D. and I first joined Delta Company, all the bunkers were dug deep into the sides of the hill. When the Monsoon Rains came, it would rain up to 120 inches each time. Each Monsoon lasted about three months and came twice a year. That meant that it rained six months a year and rained about two hundred and forty inches during a six-month period!! Sometimes the bunkers would cave in from all that rain and bury whoever was inside, sometimes suffocating them.

I built my mortar pit and bunker above ground using hundreds of sandbags. I sent my men to supply to bring all the sandbags they could carry while I scouted the hill gathering anything I could find to use to build my bunker. I made the walls three bags thick so a sniper bullet wouldn't penetrate them. I confiscated a bridge timber from the "Sea Bee" unit who was building a bridge over the stream just below our hill. I laid the bridge timber on top of the front and back walls of my bunker and spread a large tent I found over the timber and the sandbag walls. I then staked down the corners. I met a marine driving a "mule". A mule was a small gasoline powered flatbed vehicle used to transport ammo, c-rats and all kinds of gear. He was loaded with empty wooden artillery boxes headed back to the supply tent. I rerouted him to my hooch and we unloaded them.

I walked down the hill where the Sea Bees were repairing the bridge. I talked to the Sgt. in charge, and he told me he had some spare boards and agreed to haul them up the hill for me. When I got back to the top of the hill, my men had a huge stack of sandbags filled. I stacked them in a pattern similar to the way we stacked hay back home, two bags long ways with one crossways. When the walls were about six feet high, I stacked the end and front wall a few layers higher, tapering them to form a "peak" for the roof so it would shed water. The bridge timber, when laid long ways formed the ridge row. I left a small opening in the rear of the bunker and a small one leading from our living quarters into the gun pit. I did this so that when we received a fire mission, we could enter the gun pit from the living quarters without being exposed to sniper fire. The large tent I draped over the entire bunker eliminated the chance of light escaping from our bunker and lowering the chances of receiving sniper fire. I hung two ponchos over the two small doorways for the same reason.

Our bunker was about seven feet wide and about ten feet long to the front wall. The bridge timber I confiscated reached far enough past the front wall to extend out over the gun pit. I built the gun pit in a half circle pattern and about four feet high so I would be able to fire the mortar at least ninety degrees left and right. I built the front wall low enough so that I could lean the gun forward for maximum range. The large tent I draped over the entire bunker allowed us to stand our watch inside the gun pit without getting drenched to the bone when it was raining. It was a great bunker. Now, when we weren't out on patrol, we could get in out of the cold rain to sleep and whoever was on watch in the mortar pit would be underneath the tent as well.

I had my team wreck out all the wooden ammo cases I confiscated, and save the nails. I built a "three tiered" bunk bed on the west wall of the bunker. One was just above the ground, and the next two about two feet above the other. Although there were five of us in the team, two of us were always on watch, day and night. That meant the other three could lie down and try to sleep or rest somewhere other than in a foxhole half full of muddy water. I used the rest of the wood crates to build a wooden floor inside the living quarters of the bunker.

It was, by far, the best bunker on the hill. We had "all the comforts of home"! We could even light a candle at night or smoke a cigarette without cupping our hands over the end of it to avoid drawing sniper fire. I had built it so that no light could escape and be seen by the gooks lurking and waiting for the chance to shoot us from the tree line at the bottom of our hill. It was great to be able to stay relatively dry for a change while we slept or ate our C's. The cans didn't even fill up with rain before we finished eating them.

We finally got rid of the rats, scorpions and snakes that we had in all the other bunkers we had lived in. I even built a makeshift picture board and hung it on the wall so some of the guys could hang up the pictures of their girl friends they received in the mail. One of my men got a Christmas tree from home about one foot tall. We set the little tree on an ammo box in the middle of our bunker and decorated it with whatever we could find. Of course, we had no gifts to exchange, but the ones of us, who were there, were still alive and that, in itself, was a really special gift. We thanked God every day for that gift.

Everyone on the hill seemed to congregate in my bunker.

The sign says, "God bless this house. It's the only one we got".
It shows the bunker on Hill 55 that I built and draped the tent over.

None of them had the initiative to build their own, so they just gathered in mine. Sometimes after I had stood my watch in the gun pit, I could not even get inside my bunker because there were so many people in there. I continued to stand watch even though I was section leader and didn't have to. I never asked my men to do anything I wouldn't do myself. They came to my bunker to play poker, write letters home or just to visit because we were able to burn the candles inside the bunker and they couldn't. One night while I was standing my watch, a thought occurred to me. My bunker was full of people, so I decided to thin them out a little. I have always been bad about playing jokes on people or scaring them.

While I was on watch, I carefully unscrewed the top of a hand grenade and removed the blasting cap. I used my knife to scrape all the explosive powder out of the grenade, but left the fuse detonator and the "spoon" attached. When you pull the pin on a grenade, the spoon flies and the fuse detonator ignites the blasting cap, which in turn, causes the grenade to explode. The fuse detonator makes a loud "pop" a little louder than a firecracker. There were so many in my bunker I could not get inside. I told them all to *get out!* *"Go to your own bunkers"*. No one made a move to leave. I made my way around to the back of my bunker where the small door was. I sat down on an ammo crate we used for chairs, just inside the back door. I was acting really despondent and down and talking about how I was ready to end this whole damn mess. I took the grenade from my flack jacket that I had rigged earlier and was holding and handling it. A few of the guys were talking to me and trying to console me and were concerned about the way I was talking. Then all at once I said "aw F—k *it*" and pulled the pin on the grenade and let the spoon fly. When that fuse popped, my bunker "exploded" with people!! I had purposely sat in the doorway, so they couldn't get out, but that was a mistake. Those guys went out the front of the bunker and out the back of it. They ran over me going out the back door!! After they all got outside the bunker and waited for the explosion that never came, and heard me laughing my ass off, they were "pissed"! Some of them wanted to kill me and some just wanted to whip my ass, but none of them could so they just went back to their own hooches. It was funny to me but not them. I got my bunker back anyway, at least for the rest of that night.

Sometimes the gooks would succeed in overrunning a position or a small group of marines and if they didn't kill all of them, they took the others prisoner. I had heard of the ones that were taken prisoner and I vowed early on that I would never allow them to take me alive. If they didn't kill me during the assault, I would force them to kill me afterward. We found several bodies of the marines who were taken prisoner. The gooks would cut off their heads and place it on their own chests, then leave the bodies on a trail where they knew we would find them. As if that wasn't bad enough, the gooks would stick bamboo stakes in their eyes and ears. They cut off the marines' genitals, put them inside their mouth and sewed their lips shut with bamboo slivers. You cannot imagine how mutilated some of the bodies were that they left for us to find. After finding marines in this condition, we considered anything we did to them as justified in our minds. We forgot the meaning of cruel or ruthless, we had revenge and justice in our minds and hearts. They mutilated the bodies of our men beyond recognition thinking it would demoralize us or scare us into laying down our weapons and stop fighting. It worked exactly the opposite. It made us mad as hell and gave us a desire to kill the bastards who did these terrible things. I know it convinced me that I would never be taken alive. I won't go into detail about the things we did to them in retaliation. Some of the things are way too "graphic and gory", and I know none who read this would ever be able lo understand. We just felt the "insatiable desire" to kill all of them and attain some sense of balance.

There was one platoon sergeant; I think he was in third platoon that wanted a "silver star" so bad he could taste it. He told everyone he wanted one. He was a very good marine, but he was so obsessed with winning that Silver Star, he let it affect his reasoning and good judgment. When we would get ambushed on patrol or receive sniper fire, we all instinctively hit the deck and returned fire. Not this guy. He would stand straight up and try to locate the ambushers. If he saw where it was coming from, he would charge straight at them. He took way too many chances and some of the time; it wasn't only his life he was risking. He led countless patrols when I was with him and he seldom ever followed the route we plotted on the maps. No one knew where we were, so if we got into more trouble than we could handle, we could not expect reinforcements. I went on one three-day patrol with him and took one mortar team. We were supposed to maneuver out about three thousand meters to the top of a hill at a predesignated coordinance. We were to stay on this hilltop for three days and nights and report any enemy activity or movement along the valley floors on each side of this hill. We were to radio the information back to base and if we detected any enemy movement, headquarters would call in air strikes on them. These valleys were suspected Viet Cong supply routes carrying supplies farther south from the North.

Since he was leading the patrol, we didn't expect him to do what he was ordered to do. He decided on his own that we would venture farther out than the three thousand meters. We went out over six thousand meters!!! That is almost five miles from where we were supposed to be. We traveled down to where the two valleys ran together and formed one. He thought we would have a better chance of finding some gooks that way. Was he ever right!! Not only did these two trails in these two valleys come together here, but also two more from another direction ended here. Third Platoon had twelve men in it, so counting my five-man team; we had seventeen marines on this patrol. We caught one group of Viet Cong on the trail from the west completely by surprise. We killed eleven of them before they knew what hit them. The rest of them ran into the heavy underbrush. They must have had a designated time to meet other gooks here, because about that time approximately fifteen VC appeared on the trail from the North, and about the same number on the trail from the East. They almost caught us by total surprise. Now we had nowhere to go, so all we could do was stand and fight. We called for artillery support and air strikes but hell, headquarters didn't even know our location and it is hard to plot a coordinance on a map when things are that crazy.

All I can say is, it was a good thing for us that the VC liked to hit us hard and fast. They tried to inflict as many casualties as possible then retreat and run for cover. Had they realized they had us out numbered three or four to one, they would have surely over powered us and killed us all. The only thing that saved us was an M-60 Machine gunner and my mortar. The machine gunner was tearing the hell out of them and keeping them pinned down and preventing them from charging our position. I slammed my mortar into the ground and told my ammo humpers to open all the canisters of mortar rounds we had. I was hand holding the mortar tube, so as soon as they got all the ammo opened and laid out, I told my A-gunner and one ammo man to start dropping rounds down that tube and not to stop until they were all expended. I had to hold the mortar tube almost straight up in the air, because the gooks were so close to us. That made the rounds come down almost on top of us. I aimed the tube from one of the trails they were on to the other as my men kept dropping the mortar rounds down the hot, smoking tube. I am pretty sure that the shrapnel from my mortar caused some of our wounds, but had we not had the mortars, none of us would have been alive today. After it was all over and the gooks that were able broke and ran, some of our men said my team must have had ten or fifteen mortar rounds in the air at the same time! When they started hitting the ground and exploding, things got a little haywire. We rounded up our dead and wounded and located our position on the map. Then called for choppers. Needless to say, this Platoon Sergeant never got his Silver Star. Instead, he got busted to PFC and sent to Headquarters Company to finish his tour as a company clerk. I wished sometimes they had sent me with him!!!! He was lucky they didn't court martial him and send him to Fort Leavenworth for a long time.

When we went on night ambushes or LP's (Listening Posts), we would leave the hill just before sundown. We located the most likely avenues of approach that the VC would take to attack our hill and settle in for the night. We would spread out about twenty yards from each other, just close enough so it would be hard for a gook to sneak between us undetected. Also, to prevent one grenade from killing more than one of us at a time. We would crawl back into the thick underbrush a few feet off the trails. The true feeling of really being alone creeps up on you during these times. It grips you so tight you have to strain in order to breathe. But then when you can breathe, you don't want to breathe too loudly. Your heart is beating so loud, it echoes in your ears, and seems like it could be heard miles away. Your every movement makes a rustling sound that seems as though it is being broadcast on a loud speaker. So, needless to say, when we were on a night ambush or an LP, we didn't move around much. Even when we detected the movement of the VC moving down the trail, we dared not move or make a sound. It seemed as though about then is always when the mosquitoes, snakes, leeches and other insects got the worse.

When the sweat ran into our eyes and burned like gasoline, we dared not make an effort to wipe it out. All we could do was shut our eyes as tight as possible and hope to goodness our ears didn't fail us. We also hoped that we could focus once we did open them and the fighting began. We were ordered to avoid a firefight whenever possible and let the enemy pass us by, then report their strength and direction of travel the next day. This was because there was only five or six of us on the LP, and there may be as many as thirty gooks on the move. They must have been able to smell us the way we could smell them, because more times than not they would locate our position and all hell would break loose.

We always planned an escape route before we settled in for those long lonely nights. Just in case. A well-rounded plan doesn't always stay together when all hell breaks loose and bullets are flying everywhere and you know you are out numbered ten to one. No one from the hill can help either, because if they should come out to help us, we may shoot them or they might shoot us in the darkness.

Delta Company provided security for a wooden bridge across the stream at the bottom of our hill. The bridge was on the road leading out to Alpha and Bravo Company's locations. The gooks were always trying to blow this bridge up. They would float down the stream on homemade rafts at night. We killed nine of them during seven different attempts to blow up the bridge in the few short months we were on Hill 55. A command post was set up on the West end of the bridge and on the South side of the road. A tank battery was on the East end of the bridge and on the South side of the road. A machine gun bunker was located on the East end and on the North side of the road.

This photo is of the bridge over the stream we provided security for. The smoke in the background is marking for an air strike.

J.D. and I, along with a Mexican from one of my gun teams were set up and would provide security from an old Buddhist temple on the West end of the bridge and on the North side of the road. There was a "Pagoda" just outside the doorway leading into the temple. The front of the temple had long since been blown away by a tank or something, so we filled sandbags and stacked them in the opening. The interior walls were made of stucco and it had a cement floor. The roof was oriental slate, and in its day, must have been a beautiful temple.

1 -

This was the Budhist Temple we were in. Notice the sandbag wall and slate roof. The guy inside is standing where I dove out the apeture that night.

One day they called for "two bodies", which meant they wanted two people to ride shotgun on a resupply convoy to Alpha and Bravo Companies. Rather than calling some of my men off the hill, I volunteered and took J.D. with me. There were only three of us in the temple, so that left the young Mexican there to stand guard. The convoy went and came without any excitement, and we arrived back to our location. Hot, dusty and tired. It took us most all of the day.

When J.D. and I walked into the old temple, there were four or five gook kids inside going through all our stuff. When they saw us, they scattered like rats. The Mexican I had left on watch, decided to go across the road visiting and left our position unguarded.

When the kids scattered, we caught one of them. We wanted to scare them so bad they would never want to come back and steal things. The kid acted like he could not understand English, but we knew he could. We had C-Rats, books, cameras and a battery operated radio in the temple. We also had boxes of grenades, and live ammo stacked everywhere. We sure didn't want the VC to have any of that stuff, and had we not returned, they would have had all of it.

We turned the kid lose and he ran back to the village he came from about seventy-five meters east of the temple. It was located right on the banks of the large stream that the bridge crossed over. After a quick inventory, we discovered several things missing. We were mad as hell, but I should have been mad at the Mexican for leaving his post. We threw caution to the wind and did a really stupid thing. We ignored all the rules and all our training and headed for the village where the kids had come from!! Another one of my men from the hill came up just then and he went with us. He was from Staten Island New York and didn't have a lick of sense. He didn't know the meaning of the word fear but you could depend on him when things got rough.

Biggs, J.D. and I headed to the village without authorization, and without telling anyone else where we were going. When we entered the village and started going from one grass hut to another, I realized just how stupid we really were. We were acting like "John Wayne", kicking things over and searching the huts for our gear that the kids had stolen. We should have known there was no way we would ever find any of it. When we entered some of the huts unexpectedly, there were several young healthy Vietnamese men crouched in the dark corners. They would avoid eye contact as we searched the huts. Nine times out of ten, if there are any young healthy men who are not "ARVNs" (Army of the Republic of Viet Nam) then they are definitely VC. The hair on the back of my neck stood on end and I whispered; "let's get the hell out of this village"!!

All my instincts told me not to go back out the way we came into the village, so I led the other two guys out the opposite side of the village to the bank of the large, fast flowing stream. We went down the bank of the stream, back to the bridge and circled back to the old temple. I still believe to this day, that if we had tried to leave the village the way we entered it, we would not have made it out alive. I guess after so many continuous days of constant pressure and danger, we made a poor judgmental decision. Actually it was I who made the stupid decision to enter the village in the first place. I thank God I didn't get one of those guys killed.

Thinking back the next day, over the incident that happened, we should have known something wasn't just right. The morning after we went into the village, there were two old women and a little girl, on the trail, near the temple. They were picking up limbs and sticks along the small trail leading from the temple to their village. That was nothing out of the ordinary, because they were always picking them up to use for fuel to cook with. We had barbed wire strung across the trail, but over time the gook civilians crossing over it, had mashed it down some. The next day, we were talking and thinking back and we remembered that they weren't just picking up firewood; they were picking up every single little twig and dried piece of grass. Everything that would make a sound if it was stepped on in the night.

We found out that night why they had picked up all the noise making items from the trail. J.D. and I were tired to the bone after the long bumpy convoy trip to Bravo Company, so I let him take the first watch. It lasted from sundown until midnight. At midnight, he woke me up and I stood watch until four a.m. At four, I woke the Mexican that had left his post and caused all the shit that was about to happen. I woke him up and told him it was his turn to stand watch, so he groaned and walked over to the aperture and leaned against the sandbag wall we had built. That night was unusually dark. There was a heavy cloud covering but it wasn't raining. Not even the moon or the twinkling of a star could be seen, so the night was as "dark as a coal mine".

We slept on some sandbags we had stacked in the middle of the floor of the temple. We stacked them up so we would be up out of the water on the floor when it rained, because the roof didn't hold much rain out. The roof was old and dilapidated and parts of it were gone. I had a poncho tied to the support poles of the building and stretched out over the sandbags and tied off with "com wire" (communications wire) to shed off at least some of the rain that poured in through the old roof. We commandeered some "rubber ladies", as we called them (they were actually rubber blow up mattresses) somewhere and laid them on top of the sandbags. They were great compared to sleeping directly on top of the sandbags filled with hard sand and rocks.

As long as I live, I will never know what woke me up from a dead sleep that night after my watch was over. I have to believe that God wasn't ready for me to die just yet. I believe He took hold of my foot and "shook me" awake. But something woke me. At four thirty, just thirty minutes after I woke the Mexican for his watch, I sprang awake with an awful feeling in my stomach. I looked over and the Mexican I woke up, was lying next to J.D. sound asleep!! I raised up on my elbows in a half sitting position and kicked the Mexican on the foot and woke him up again. When he opened his eyes, I said *"get your ass back on watch"*. Sleeping on watch is something that is completely unacceptable in a war zone. He rolled over, stood up and stretched, then walked back over to the small aperture and leaned on the sandbag wall. What happened next seemed like it lasted for an eternity, although it all happened in a few minutes or maybe even a few seconds.

The Mexican stood there for a few seconds, then he half turned toward me and whispered; *"Hey Tony I think"*. I guess he was going to say, *"I think there is someone out there"*, but he never got to finish his sentence. At that very moment, a hand grenade came through the small aperture where he was standing! It must have been a Russian made "chicom grenade", because during training we studied all different types of foreign made munitions. This grenade was "spewing sparks" sort of like a firecracker fuse and I knew our grenades didn't do that. Everything that happened after that moment was the "reacting" I have talked about, because I sure as hell didn't have time to think things out or at least I didn't take the time.

The Mexican I had awakened, panicked. He didn't yell "grenade" like he was supposed to do and had been trained to do over and over during basic training. Everything was a blur after that, but I jumped up from the sandbag bed and fell to the floor on my hands and knees to get the grenade. It was spewing and bouncing around on the slick cement floor. I finally found it, picked it up and threw it back out the aperture it had just come through. While I was still on my knees, another God Damn grenade came through the window!!! I knew I had to throw it back outside the aperture or it would kill all three of us. I finally found the grenade and was about to throw it back outside. Just then the Mexican ran over me and knocked me down. He was running to the other side of the room where the only door leading outside the temple was. I lost my grip on the grenade and dropped it. Desperation set in I guess, I remember thinking; "I *only have seven seconds to find it*". During all our training we learned that our fragmentation grenades have a seven second fuse. Once you let the spoon fly, you have seven seconds to get rid of it. I knew my seven seconds had to be up.

When I couldn't find the second grenade, I got up, stepped up on a bench in front of the other aperture and screamed "*grenade*" as loud as I could. I started to dive outside the building. Just as I dove, the grenade exploded directly underneath the bench I was standing on. I guess the heavy wooden bench absorbed most of the fragmentation from the grenade, or it would have surely killed me. I only caught a few pieces in my back and in the backs of my legs. We ate, slept and lived with our flack jackets on, and I thank God I had mine on this night. The flack jacket absorbed or deflected a huge amount of the red-hot shrapnel from the grenade that would have been inside me, had I not had it on. It was shredded to pieces. They were hot and really heavy, but I am glad I slept in it that night.

I am holding two flak jackets, one is good and the other one I had on the night in the church.

When the grenade blew me out of the window, I landed in a pile of C-Ration cans. After we ate the C's, we just threw the cans outside the apertures. We figured they would help us detect anyone sneaking up on me. I guess we should have thrown some out the other side too!! Just as I landed in the cans, an automatic weapon opened up on me from the village. It was probably a "Russian made AK-47". They have a distinct sound of their own and that was the weapon of choice for the gooks. The bullets from the AK were "tearing up jack"! They were knocking the cans up all around me and sparks were flying everywhere. I realized instantly that I had to get out of there and get behind some cover. I jumped up to run for cover and at that moment a third grenade exploded inside the temple. The concussion from it blew the sandbag wall we had built, outwards and right on top of me! I thought, "*Oh shit*"! I kicked the sandbags off of me, jumped up and ran behind the pagoda outside the small doorway leading into the temple.

All at once, reality slapped me right in the face! Those bastards had to be standing just on the other side of the building from me and here I am without a weapon, once more. There hadn't been time for me to grab a rifle when I had "exited the building". Then I realized that J.D. and the Mexican were still inside the temple, or at least I thought so at that moment. I remember thinking, "*Oh God please don't let them be dead*".

J.D. had become "my little brother". He may have been closer to me than my own brothers. These were my men; my team and I didn't want to lose any of them, not now, not ever.

The automatic weapon was still firing and tearing up everything around me. I decided this isn't worth a damn, so I ran the few steps toward the building and dove inside the doorway. J.D. had stumbled around and found his rifle and he almost shot me when I came diving through the door. He thought I was the gook coming after him. He was in total shock, because he was sound asleep when all this hell broke loose. He couldn't hear a thing because of the concussion from the grenades. I asked him if he was okay, but he couldn't hear me. Just then another Goddamn grenade came through the same window!! J.D. had his back to the window and not being able to hear, he was totally unaware of it. I grabbed him by the front of his flack jacket and shoved him outside the door and over to one side of it up against the wall of the building. After the grenade exploded inside, I thought to myself that those bastards had to be on the other side of the building, standing next to the window and just lobbing those grenades through it.

At that very moment, all the fear and confusion inside of me turned into rage. I grabbed J.D.'s rifle from him and fired back at the muzzle flashes of the AK-47 in the village until the flashes stopped. Then I slammed another magazine into J.D.'s rifle and ran around to the back of the temple and stopped at the corner. By this time, everyone on the hill was aware that something bad was happening down below, so someone, probably one of mortar crews, fired some illumination rounds into the cold black sky. I peeped around the corner of the building and I could see two gooks standing beside the window that the grenades had come through, with their backs up against the wall. One of them held a sack of some kind and was handing the other one more grenades. There was a third gook lying dead on the ground a few feet away. Evidently, one of the grenades I had thrown back out the window had killed him. I stepped around the corner and killed the other two with J.D.'s rifle.

Just then, the illumination burned out and every sound on earth fell silent except for the pounding of my own heart! It felt as though my heart would explode inside my chest. The whole valley developed an "eerie" look after they fired some more illumination into the air. It burned with a brilliant bright light and seemed to be suspended in time hanging up there in the sky. They moved ever so slightly from side to side as they floated to earth on small parachutes, then burned out. The shadows they created seem to dance in the darkness. Then there was that total silence again and the darkest dark I have ever known thus far.

Fear was knocking on my door once more! I didn't know if there were any more gooks close by or not. I ran back around the building to the other side where J.D. was still standing frozen up against the wall of the building. I had fired all the ammunition J.D. had, so I knew I had to go back inside the church and find my own weapon. I pulled J.D. back inside the doorway and began feeling my way through the rubble and finally found my rifle and cartridge belt with all my ammo in it. We rummaged through the devastation the grenades had caused until we found his cartridge belt, and then we waited!!!

Finally, after what seemed to be a lifetime, reinforcements came. They took over for us and we went to the command post where a corpsman was waiting to treat our wounds. Somehow, miraculously, J.D. only had one small piece of shrapnel from the grenades just below his left elbow, plus, he still couldn't hear a thing. The only explanation we could think of was that the first grenade that blew me out the aperture, also blew him off the sandbags and he had stayed glued to the floor when the others had exploded. That is the only thing that saved his life, because as I mentioned, the walls of the temple were made of a "stucco" material. There was not one square inch on the walls that had not been torn to bits by the shrapnel. My ears were ringing to "high heaven" so I'm sure J.D.'s were too. I had been in "pretty close proximity" to the explosions too. I didn't know at that moment, but my ears would ring and roar for the rest of my life. They do to this day.

At sunrise, when we returned to the temple, we discovered a "homemade bomb" lying on top of the sandbags where we slept. It was a C-Ration can full of TNT. For some reason, it had not detonated. If it had we would all be dead. It would have leveled the Temple. Anyway, we were taken to the command post.

When we walked inside the tent, the Mexican was sitting on an ammo box smoking a cigarette. I stopped in my tracks and the realization hit me like a ton of bricks that *"this mother fucker almost got me and J.D. killed"*!! I knew at that moment that he had run out on us and left us to die. I completely lost it. I kicked him in the chest as hard as I could and before he hit the ground, I was sitting on top of him. I had my "K-Bar" (a marine combat knife) to his throat. I always kept it razor sharp. I was shaking all over and had every intention of killing him right then and right there. I don't know why I didn't kill him at that instant, but I didn't. The Mexican was screaming, crying and begging me not to kill him. The CO was screaming at me. J.D. was screaming at me, hell everyone was screaming except me! The Mexican begged me not to kill him and told me that he was scared to death when the grenade came inside with us and that was the reason he ran out on us. I was still sitting on his chest with my knife to his throat with every intention of killing him. I told him that he couldn't have been a damn bit more scared than I was, but that I would never run out on anybody.

Reconstructing the events in our minds, we figured that after I threw the first grenade back out the window and the second one came in, he ran for the door. He panicked and all he could think of was to get out of the building. That is when he ran over me and knocked me down and I dropped the second grenade. He ran on out the door and into the tangled barbed wire around our position. The sling of his rifle got caught up in the barbed wire, so he left his rifle there and ran again! All of this happened before the automatic weapon opened up on us or they would have surely killed the Mexican when he went outside the building.

A few weeks later they awarded J.D. and me "Purple Hearts" for "wounds received in action"! When they told me that the Mexican was going to get a Purple Heart too, I blew up once more. The only wounds the Mexican had were the cuts he got from the tangled consentina wire while he was running out on us. I told the CO that if they gave this Mother Fucker a Purple Heart, they could keep mine and that I would kill him like I should have done that night in the command post tent. I told them he should be shot for running out on us because that would definitely qualify as "cowardice in the face of the enemy". According to the UCMJ (uniform code of military justice), he should be shot by a firing squad. So, as it happened we got Purple Hearts and the Mexican didn't. They took him out of my mortar team and transferred him to Bravo Company the next day. I don't know if he made it home from Viet Nam or not. I honestly don't care.

This is the front wall and roof after the grenades exploded in the the temple. We slept just on the other side of the remaining sandbags

This is the "after" showing the destruction the hand grenades caused. The 4x4 is what I stepped up on to dive out of the aperture, and the c-ration cans are where I landed.

Some weeks after all this happened, Delta Company was the main "blocking force" for a major operation, and for the life of me, I can't recall the name of it. We were to disperse our entire company along a designated line just outside "death valley". This was the lush green valley I had noticed and thought was so beautiful the first day I arrived on Hill 55 with the truck convoy from Danang. The gooks controlled this area, and we had been warned that it was "infested" with them. This operation was designed to clear them out of this area. There were numerous punji pits like the one I had encountered, and everything you touched was booby-trapped. The gooks were masters at booby-trapping things. Hell, we thought they could even booby trap a sheet of paper. We were warned not to pick up any souvenirs or anything we found lying around.

We set up just inside the tree line facing a relatively open area about two hundred meters out in front of us. We dug our foxholes about fifty meters apart and waited, one man to each foxhole. Some other unit, I can't remember which one, was flown by "Chinook Helicopters" (huge double bladed helicopters) to a point approximately five thousand meters to the south of us.

This unit had tanks; "auntose vehicles" (this was a track vehicle with six-106 recoilless rifles mounted on it) and "Huey" helicopter gun ships. These things were awesome. They were loaded with firepower and could fly ninety-five miles an hour at tree top level. This was a "major operation" and one of the very few "free fire zones" we ever encountered. Free fire zone meant; "if it moves, kill it"!!

There were way too many rules and regulations we had to abide by and every one of them prevented us from fighting this war the way it should have been fought, to win it! The "Commandant of the Marine Corps" told the President that he would win this war in sixty days if he would allow it. The entire country was only slightly larger than the state of California. The Commandant said he would put all American forces in Viet Nam on line and "sweep" the country from Saigon to Hanoi. The people with the authority to let him do this and end the war wouldn't have it. They were all too busy filling their pockets. They tried to run this war from behind a desk in Washington.

All the villagers, or so-called civilians in this area were warned and given time to evacuate, so anyone left would be considered the enemy and fair game. The other unit got set up and organized and initiated their move toward our position. They would be the "driving force". It sort of reminded me of hunting pheasant back home. Several of us would spread out on line in a corn or Milo field and walk down the rows to the other end. There would be more hunters at the other end called blockers. As we, the driving force walked, the pheasants that didn't fly up and get shot by us, would run ahead of us to the ends of the rows. As the two groups of hunters got closer and closer together, the running pheasants had nowhere to go. Some of the pheasants would "stick" and hide under weeds until we literally stepped on top of them. When that happened, and they finally flushed, it would scare the crap out of you. But the majority of them would run ahead of the driving force to the ends of the rows and more times than not, there were too many of them for the blocking force to shoot.

This operation was supposed to take three to five days, depending on how much resistance the driving force encountered and how bad the weather was. That isn't much time because after all, five thousand meters is a long way, when you consider that they would be traveling through dense undergrowth, and rice paddies while doing battle every step of the way. They didn't dare travel too fast lest they bypass a large number of the gooks who would stick, like the scared pheasants that hid under the weeds. Some of them would duck out to one side or the other.

We had been dug in for about three or four hours and had a meal of cold C's and were preparing for what we knew would be one hell of a battle once the driving force drove the gooks to us. I left my mortar on the hill. We could only have one marine to the foxhole, because we only had one Company covering the same area that should have had two Companies. We were set up in an area where intelligence determined would be the main retreat or escape route the gooks would take in order to avoid making contact with the driving force.

We could hear the sounds of battle in the far distance and knew there was fierce fighting going on. We could see the smoke from the "Willie Peter" rounds, marking enemy targets, rising to "Heavenly heights" in the clear blue sky. The driving force called for air strikes ahead of them, and we knew it had begun. We were on full alert facing the clearing with the jungle to our backs.

For some strange reason, a feeling of urgency came over me as I sat there full of anticipation and wondering what this day held in store for me. I got this feeling like some people get when they think someone is watching them. I turned to look into the trees behind me only to see a gook kid maybe twelve or thirteen years of age. Before I could even think to ask him what he was doing here, he pulled the pin on a grenade and threw it right into my foxhole with me. He turned to run back into the jungle, but before he took two steps, I instinctively shot him four times as I half jumped and half rolled outside my foxhole. I am fortunate, that when a grenade explodes, it blows up and out, instead of sideways. After I shot the kid, I lay as flat to the ground as possible for that endless "seven seconds". The walls of the foxhole absorbed almost all the shrapnel that didn't pass over me. I only caught a couple of pieces in my shoulder. Those pieces penetrated and tore through my flack jacket just above the fiberglass plates.

A flack jacket has four-inch by six-inch, Teflon plates sewn into layers of strong canvas. They are designed to deflect fragmentation and even some bullets from an angle. If a bullet was fired from long range and had lost most of its velocity when it hit you, the jacket would usually slow the bullet down enough that it wouldn't kill you. It would not stop or deflect a bullet fired at close range. They were heavy, hot and "bundlesom", but they saved a bunch of marines' lives that had them on at the right time.

Other than the time Dave West got killed, this incident changed me more than anything else that happened to me while I was in Viet Nam, or ever in my lifetime for that matter. It worked on my mind like nothing ever had. I almost lost my mind.

After my senses came back to me, and my brain half way returned to normal, I looked at the small body lying dead at my feet. This was just a kid; a little boy and I had just killed him!! I puked up what C-Rations I had just eaten and all the liquid in my stomach. As I mentioned, I almost lost my mind. I couldn't eat, I couldn't sleep and it was about to drive me crazy. The Chaplain tried to talk to me, and console me but couldn't. After many long torturous hours of crying, talking and praying he finally made me see that this kid could have killed me just as dead as if he had been fifty years old. He convinced me that the kid's age hadn't mattered and that he was the enemy. He was there to kill me and almost succeeded. I finally accepted the fact that if he was that intent on killing me, that this kid had probably killed marines before. I accepted it and admitted that he would have killed more, had I not killed him. He was willing to die in order to kill me. All of this helped immensely, but I still had nightmares for years to come. We killed kids his age several times on night ambushes that were setting land mines and booby traps. We even killed a gook one night that had been shaving us with a straight razor for three months!! They had let him set up a make shift barbershop inside our perimeter! We just never knew who the enemy was.

Whoever planned and organized this operation we were involved in knew what they were doing! When the driving force reached a point several hundred yards to our front, there were gooks coming at our position in droves!!! Like the pheasants, they had nowhere to go. We realized in a hurry that we needed a lot more troops for the blocking force. We shot up every round of ammunition we had brought with us which was thousands of rounds each. We killed more VC and NVA on this operation than any single operation that I can recall except during the "Siege of Khe Sahn". There were dead bodies everywhere. We had caught them completely off guard. They had no idea we were set up and dug in as a blocking force to prevent their retreat. They thought they could just attack and retreat at their own pace, moving ahead of the slow advancement of the driving force and disappear back into the jungle like they always did. They would usually post a few snipers to fire a few shots at the main columns of our patrols while the rest of them made a "hasty retreat" to their hide-a-ways. This went down in history as one of the bloodiest and fiercest battles of the war.

Later the CO sent a replacement to my foxhole and he told me to report to the CO's area and stay with his radioman. He said he wanted me there in case we needed to call in an artillery barrage, but I knew why he wanted me there even though the incident with the kid was never mentioned.

The operation lasted the full five days. After it was over, we were supposed to be flown back to Hill 55 for a few days of rest. We were all worn to a frazzle and exhausted after such fierce and continuous fighting, for such a long, sustained period of time. We had no rest and very little sleep for five days and nights. Instead of loading up on the choppers as planned, for a short safe ride back to the hill, our plans were about to change. Some "boot lieutenant" made the suggestion that one of the platoons should make a wide sweep back to our hill in order to pick up any "stragglers" who may have dodged the driving force of the operation.

It was about four thousand meters back to the hill, but that was "as the crow flies". The CO thought that was a good idea, so they plotted a return route on the maps. This route would take us on a little "six thousand meter trek" back to the hill through rice paddies, and jungle. Delta Company had suffered the least number of casualties, since we had been the blocking force, so we were nominated as the lucky ones to make the sweep. There were no roads where we were going so if we should need more ammo, water, or any kind of supplies, they would have to be flown to us by chopper.

As I have said, this area, approximately twenty-five square miles, was infested with the Viet Cong. The other companies flew back in helicopters. As the last sounds of their departure faded away, we saddled up and headed out on our "mop-up" campaign. During the first three thousand meters or so through the muck and mud of the rice paddies, we got hit three times. The temperature nudged the one hundred and twenty five mark and there wasn't a breath of air. We were loaded down with full combat gear and all the water and ammo we could carry. I felt like a packhorse.

The gooks must have known which route we would take because when they ambushed us, they would let the point man walk through and then hit us from both sides and from the front. There were definitely more than just a few stragglers in this area. After the third time we got hit, we were all running low on ammo, so we located a clearing and set up in a defensive position around it. We called on the radio for more supplies.

The gooks shot down three helicopters trying to reach our position. The Battalion Commander made the decision that it was too costly to keep trying to get to us in this location. He gave the orders for us to fight our way on east another seventeen hundred meters to a place on his map. We were cut off from any chance of resupply or reinforcements. The gooks figured out the predicament we were in so they hit us hard. I thought they would over run us at any moment, but we fought them back.

We saddled up and headed east, using the trees as cover and a safe haven of sorts. We traveled a short distance and came to a village that had a stream running past it. The stream was only about ten feet deep but it was forty or fifty feet wide and flowing pretty fast. As we tried to get everyone across the stream, snipers hit us from the village. We called in artillery and counter attacked the village and took control of it. We stayed inside this village fighting for our lives for three days and two nights. By the third day, we were almost completely out of ammunition.

Our food and water supply we started out with, was depleted completely. The water was no problem; we drank the water from the stream. It was moving water, so it wasn't too stagnant. We carried "iodine" to purify water like this anyway. It tasted something awful, but it kept us from getting malaria and a whole host of other diseases. Third platoon was positioned in the village. First and second platoons were dispersed along the stream back to the West. Fourth platoon moved out into the tree line North of the village.

We were all really hungry by this time. We hadn't noticed it so much during the wild commotion of getting ambushed and attacked, but now things had settled down a little. I decided to do a "recon" of the village and see what I could find. Most of the guys from the big cities and the Yankees in our unit knew nothing about survival. The villagers had left some old chickens in a coop when they departed. The chickens were infested with lice or something. Almost all the feathers had come off of them. We pulled off the chickens' heads and skinned them because we didn't want to eat the skin. I boiled them in my "piss pot" (that is the steel part of my helmet) with water from the stream. We had no salt or seasoning but it tasted as good as "KFC" to us. We also found some rice in straw baskets inside some of the hooches. We picked out all the bugs and leeches that we could and I boiled it in my helmet too. We ate it like it was good!! I figured that the boiling water would sterilize any bugs left in the rice.

Someone told me they had found a pig at the outskirts of the village, so we went to investigate. That was the "ugliest" pig I have ever seen. It was and old sow, no telling how old she was. She looked like she had delivered twenty litters of pigs. She was really skinny and real "sway-backed". She had developed a bad case of "mange", so she hardly had any hair left. We decided we would kill her and eat her.

I had a gunner from Staten Island New York. He was the one

74

who went into the village with J.D. and me when the kids stole our gear. He decided he would be the one to kill her so we could eat her. He started shooting this old pig in the stomach with a .45 caliber pistol! This is what I meant about Yankees and survival. The old sow just squealed real loud and ran around the pen. He would have probably never killed her shooting her in the stomach. I finally told him to put that pistol away. I got inside the pen with the old pig. I shot her between the eyes and cut her throat with my K-Bar. I made the cut large enough to stick my hand inside the gash. I reached down inside her throat and sliced her heart open so she would bleed out good. That is the way we learned to do it at home, growing up, when we slaughtered our own hogs. All the neighbors would gather at our house once a year to kill hogs, because we had the only "scalding vat" in the county. We ate really well that night.

The leeches were terrible here, I guess because we were so close to this stream. They were real ugly little creatures. After every patrol, especially night patrols or LPs, (when we would crawl back into the underbrush, and stay all night), we would be covered in them. When we returned to the hill, we would strip off all our clothes, if we had the time, and burn the leeches off of each other's backs and places we couldn't see on ourselves. These things were tiny little "worm looking" creatures until they attached themselves to your skin. Once they got their "suckers" into us and started sucking out our blood, they increased in size tremendously. The more blood they sucked out of us, the bigger they got. That was why it was so important to get them off of us as soon as possible after we discovered them. If they went undetected for a long while, they could grow as big as a small cigar, and they would be full of our blood. I have had as many as thirty of them on me at one time! You should never pull a leech off when they have their head buried in you skin. We would touch a lit cigarette to one of them, and they would withdraw their heads and then we could kill them. They couldn't stand salt either. If we had any table salt from our

75

C-rations, available, we would sprinkle salt on them and they would start writhing around and blood would come out all their pores, our blood! We got most of them on us around streams when we were filling our canteens with drinking water, on patrols or shaving when we got the chance.

We received orders to evacuate the village ASAP! Intelligence reports said the gooks were mounting a major offensive on our position from all directions. We found a small wooden boat that had been carved out of a large tree trunk. We started transporting men across the stream, four at a time in the boat. It was too deep, too wide and too swift to cross it any other way. Finally, as the last four of us were crossing the stream, they hit us hard from the tree line on the other side of the village. They didn't charge us, so we fought them back and disappeared into the trees and distanced ourselves from them before they could cross the stream. We made our way back to a road we located on the map and linked up with reinforcements coming to help us, with food, water and more ammo.

We were still a long way from the hill and this road didn't lead us there. We mapped out a route of travel so that we would avoid the thickest part of the jungle and headed out. We almost made it back to the hill with only a few sniper rounds. When we were within five hundred meters of the hill, and we could even see it, we got hit once again. We were all hot, exhausted, mad and really tired of this shit. This time, when they ambushed us, instead of "hitting the deck" and returning fire as we usually did, some of those crazy marines began to yell as loud as they could. They yelled while firing at the gooks and charged, straight into the ambush! It must have surprised or scared the hell out of those gooks. The firing from the tree line stopped almost instantly and the ambush ended.

Afterwards we were all standing around talking and caring for our wounded when "it happened"! We were standing way too close together. This was one of those "lax moments" I mentioned that you avoid at all costs. There was at least one of the gooks that hadn't retreated or ran when the marines charged their ambush. He fired a rifle grenade of some kind amongst us. It made an "aerial burst", which means it detonated about six feet in the air, instead of exploding when it hit the ground. We all hit the deck.

Dave West was one of the "TEXICANS" in our group from Dallas. He was a grunt, but he spent a lot of his spare time at my hooch and was like a brother to me. We had talked for hours on end, late into many nights, about everything you could imagine. He had left his wife and family, as I had to come to this place. Evidently, Dave must have been directly between the rifle grenade and me when it exploded. It almost decapitated him. He was the only one killed, but it severely wounded seven more. The first thing I saw when I looked up was Dave lying next to me. His brains and blood were blown all over me!! I went berserk and nothing anyone said or did could calm me down.

I was a different man after that day. I went a little bit crazy (if I wasn't already), and would never get over it. From that moment on, I changed. I went to the Chaplain every chance I got. I prayed, but nothing helped, so I stopped going at all. I felt like I could never wash Dave's blood off of me. I couldn't eat, I couldn't sleep and I hated everything and everybody. I even hated the world. This thing had affected me much worse than killing that kid. The killing got easier after that. I loved it, I looked forward to it and that scared the hell out of me. I volunteered for every patrol, every night ambush or anything that would get me close enough to kill some more of those M fers who killed Dave! I never tried to be as quiet as I had been, on night ambushes or LP's anymore. I wanted them to find me. They had killed Dave but they would pay and pay and pay some more. I lost count of how many a long time before I left for home. Not even forty-two years has begun to heal that scar. It will never heal.

Another time before 1/26 moved north to Khe Sahn, we were deployed on ships. We boarded large navy ships of some kind and went north by way of the South China Sea. We were unloaded from the ship and onto landing craft like the ones you see on TV in the movies. We made a beachhead landing just south of the DMZ. Although we didn't encounter very heavy resistance when we landed, we still had some casualties. We fought our way through to a predesignated area on the map and regrouped approximately one thousand meters outside the DMZ. Our orders were to "expel" the NVA from the DMZ. They had been inside it for a long time, we could tell. There were permanent bunkers, mortar pits and even observation towers. They had laid minefields and booby traps for us, and the punji-pits were on every trail they thought we would travel.

Our Battalion consisted of four companies, which were Alpha, Bravo, Charlie and Delta Companies. Delta Company had the best track record, so we were given the honor of entering the DMZ first, as the spearhead of the operation. We spent the night there, and about an hour before sunrise, we saddled up and headed into the DMZ. Of course, the NVA knew we were coming, and our avenue of approach was drastically limited. They hit us with all they had. We were involved in some of the most intense fighting we had encountered in quiet a while.

We were fighting for our lives, and fought hard for several long grueling hours. We were slowly gaining ground and inching our way farther into the DMZ. The fighting wasn't the only job we had at hand. We also had the duty of clearing out mine fields, booby traps and destroying the bunkers as we went. The plan was that Delta Company would fight our way in as far as we could, then Charlie Company would advance from our rear and we would fall back. Then Bravo Company would advance, then Alpha Company, sort of "leap-frogging". By the time Charlie Company reached us, we were almost defeated.

During the transition with Charlie Company, they called for a fire mission from my mortar. My ammo humpers were breaking out rounds when a sniper zeroed in on us. The first round he fired hit my ammo man in the hollow of the throat. The bullet almost tore his head off. I yelled for someone to pinpoint the snipers' location, but no one saw the muzzle flash. His next shot missed us, but the impact of the bullet blew mud all over us and into my A-gunners' eyes so bad he couldn't see. This time, someone saw the muzzle flash from his rifle. They pointed out the tree it came from, so I readied the mortar. Before I could get off a round, he fired again. The bullet slammed into my A-gunners' arm. It hit him right in the bend of his elbow and almost took his arm off. After the bullet passed through his elbow, it hit the firing mechanism of my mortar and shattered it, just inches from my crotch. When he fired that shot, I saw the muzzle flash myself. My mortar was out of commission, so I took an M-60 machine gun from a gunner close to me and sprayed an entire belt of ammo into the tree where I had seen the muzzle flash. I not only killed that sniper, but two more fell dead from the same tree that no one had seen.

We lost a lot more men during this operation. We entered the DMZ three times and fell back three times in a period of four days and nights. Our Company Commander was a young Captain. He called Battalion Headquarters and reported that we were getting cut to pieces. He requested artillery and air support. The Colonel told him that due to the political aspects, he was not allowed to fire artillery into the DMZ and it was considered a "no fly" zone for our planes. They ordered our Captain to send us back into the DMZ to finish the job we were sent to do. Our captain blew up. He told the full bird colonel to "go f##k himself, and that if he would send the artillery, and air support we would go back in, otherwise the colonel could do it himself'. Our respect for the Captain grew after that. We started the operation with over sixteen hundred men. When we left that area, we had less than nine hundred who weren't dead or wounded.

When we boarded the ships to go on this operation, we enjoyed being taken out of harms way for a few hours. They had good, hot chow and everything was clean. When we passed through the chow line though, the stupid swabbies serving the food refused to serve us if our hands were dirty or more especially, if we were carrying our weapons. They had absolutely no concept of the way we had lived for so long, and the conditions. But when they picked us up for the return trip, things were a little bit different. We came through that chow line looking like hell. We were covered with sweat, mud and the blood from the ones who didn't make it. We had weapons slung over our shoulders and hand grenades hanging from our flack jackets. The machine gunners had belts of ammo criss-crossed across their chests. Those same stupid swabbies knew better than to utter one derogatory word to us. They served us and even asked if we wanted extra portions.

I thought about the swabbies later and admitted to myself that everyone had a certain job to do in this war, but somehow it didn't balance in my mind. These guys slept in a clean, dry and safe bed every night, and ate three hot meals every day. Their uniforms stayed clean and dry all the time. Ours in turn, rotted off of us and we slept in the muck and mud. They sat thirty miles off the coast on this ship and no one was shooting at them twenty four-seven, or sneaking up on them at night trying to cut their throats. All of this, and yet, they drew the exact same combat pay we did. They were also entitled to wear the same medals that we were fighting and dying for. Now, just think about that for a minute!!!

My brother Loyd and his wife Murlene, kept me going and helped me retain a little of my sanity. They were a major factor in giving me the will to survive and make it back home alive. They wrote to me often and sent me a lot of "care packages", as we called them. They were filled with all kinds of "goodies" from home, like cookies, foot powder and all kinds of things. We all shared our packages with each other, even though, the cookies were usually three weeks old by the time we got them. We ate them anyway! One guy even got a plastic baby bottle full of "Southern Comfort" whiskey, sometimes. It tasted great.

After Dave got killed, I stayed away from everyone as best I could. I never wanted to get close to any of these guys again. When you eat, fight, bleed and sleep in the same hole in the ground as these guys, it is hard to avoid it. By this time, I had sort of adopted J.D. as my little brother too. After I got him assigned to my mortar squad, we became really close. I hate to think what I would have done if he had gotten killed that night in the Temple. I do know one thing without a doubt. This old world would have had one less Mexican.

Once, I wrote to Loyd about how things really were and how I felt. I told him that I didn't care whether I lived or died. He kept me going with his letters. I told him I just wanted to kill them and hurt them as bad as I could and that I had some stupid feeling that I wanted to be a hero. I'll never forget what he wrote back to me. He wrote: *"Tony, to me you guys are all heroes over there"*. He and Murlene both helped me tremendously and I will never forget them for all they did for me. I still have the small, pocket-sized Bible that Murlene sent me.

A few days after we returned to our hill, while we were on another patrol, we got word that Alpha Company was under heavy attack and about to be over run. We were only about nine hundred meters from their location, so we headed toward them. We traveled as fast as we could, but we had to go through the flooded rice paddies, because we didn't dare walk up on top of the dikes. As explained, my mortar tube and base plate weighed over thirty pounds. My flack jacket, c-rations, ammo, canteens and other gear weighed heavy too. In all, I was carrying over one-hundred pounds, plus my own body weight. It was really difficult to travel very fast while sinking up over your knees in the mud. Also, while carrying all that weight, and getting shot at. All of this in one hundred and thirty degree heat. We knew we were Alpha Companies' only hope, so we did it.

After a long while, we stopped for a breather at the edge of a rice paddy. I felt as if my head would explode, I had such a headache. I was "heaving" and trying to vomit, but had nothing in my stomach. I was dehydrated like crazy from sweating so much. The corpsman sat me down on an old building foundation and gave me some water. He poured water on the back of my head to cool me off. I was resting my elbows on my knees with my face in my hands when a shot rang out. A VC sniper across the rice paddy from us caught us in one of those "lax moments". The bullet, as best we could determine, traveled over one marines' head as he bent over. It continued on and tore through another man's thigh, shattering the bone. The bullet then hit a third man in the foot and cut the tendon just above his heel. Then the bullet ricochet into my left leg beside the shinbone. That gook had lined us up pretty well.

By the time the bullet hit me, it had lost almost all of its velocity. It didn't go very deep into my leg. The corpsman extracted the bullet as I watched him. It wasn't bad, but my head was really killing me now. I was suffering from "heat exhaustion", which was bordering on a heat stroke. They loaded me on the med-evac with the wounded and flew us to the hill. The Corpsman gave me a shot of something that knocked my lights out, and I welcomed it. I didn't know anything for three days.

Just when we thought things could not get any worse, they did! Delta Company received orders to go north to "Khe Sahn"!! From all the reports we had heard about this place, Danang was a picnic. Khe Sahn is located in the northernmost part of Viet Nam. It is located between a range of mountains and a few miles east of the Laotian border. The ocean is just a few miles on to the east from there. This is one of the narrowest parts of Viet Nam. Khe Sahn lay just three miles south of the DMZ. It was on the "doorstep to North Viet Nam ".

The history books talk about the "TET OFFENSIVE" and many major battles in Viet Nam, but none of them compare to the "Siege of Khe Sahn". That was the single most bloody and costly battle of the war in American lives lost. The hills around Khe Sahn overlooked the "Ho Chi Minh Trail" which was a direct resupply trail leading from North Viet Nam to points all through the south. They used it to replenish supplies to the VC and to the NVA throughout South Viet Nam.

We left Danang about the middle of May and headed north. We flew by C-147 transport planes to some point; I think it was Hue. This place was about fifteen miles east of Khe Sahn and twenty miles south. It must have been close to the coastline, because there was a bay that led to the ocean near the airstrip. We traveled from there, farther north. We loaded up in "deuce and a half" trucks (these were two and a half ton military trucks). We traveled through Hue where another horrendous battle would be fought a few weeks later. When Hue, was destroyed, both sides lost countless numbers of men. "The Battle of Hue" is another famous battle in the history books. There was heavy sustained fighting from one building to the next. The whole city was almost completely destroyed. We left Hue and traveled toward Dong Ha.

We came to the end of any type of road that the old heavy trucks could follow, so we "saddled up" once more for a long hike. We were at a place called "the rock pile". It was located about eight or ten miles from Khe Sahn, I think, but no roads led there from here. We stayed on the rock pile for three days and helped them rebuild bunkers and string wire. They had been on the receiving end of heavy artillery fire from North Viet Nam. Our politicians back home would not allow us to bomb North Viet Nam for fear of "offending them"!! The gooks must have wanted this rocky hill pretty bad, and almost gained control of it.

We heard on the Armed Forces Radio station that "Hanoi Hanna" had broadcast that the NVA would over run our position tonight and kill every American here! She declared that they would leave our bones to bleach out in the hot sun. Hanoi Hanna was Viet Nam's version of "Tokyo Rose" from WW II. "Propaganda"?? Maybe-Maybe not. She called Delta CO. 1/26 by name and number as the ones they would annihilate, and leave our bones in the sun. She almost had us believing it after the first night there. What was to come that first night was worse than just a human wave assault of troops coming at us. Intelligence reported afterwards, that we had survived over one thousand incoming rounds of mortars and artillery from North Viet Nam and the surrounding jungles. We were really proud of our government for not allowing someone to bomb the hell out of them and stop this.

The Rock Pile was a hill about the size of four-city blocks square. When you think about it, there weren't many places to hide to avoid one thousand artillery and mortar rounds exploding inside an area that size. But try to hide we did. That was the only thing we could do. We could always fight and beat back the ambushes and the human wave attacks, but there isn't much you can do against artillery shells raining down on you from the sky. All we could do was dig in a little deeper, keep our heads down and pray that one of the shells didn't land in our holes with us.

Just before dawn, the shelling stopped and here they came. It looked and sounded as though there were thousands of them charging up the hill yelling and firing. Evidently, they must have thought the artillery had killed or wounded most of us and they weren't far from being right. The ones of us still alive threw so much shit back at them; it stopped them in their tracks about half way up the hill. They made it almost to our consentina wire twice before we beat them back. They were totally exposed and out in the open with no cover. We, on the other hand were up above them and dug in. We had foxholes and trenches we had dug for just this type of situation. I can't recall the body count of dead enemy soldiers that day, but headquarters paid the villagers at the bottom of the hill, to carry the bodies away. These troops were NVA regular soldiers, because they were in full dress uniforms. The VC in the south usually just wore silk clothes that looked like black pajamas.

The NVA Regulars were highly trained and organized, the same as we were. They were very efficient and they operated as a well-disciplined unit. Instead of a small band of gooks using guerilla tactics of hit and run like the VC in the South. If you have ever seen a war movie on television, when the enemy troops were charging up a hill at our troops, try to visualize being there in person! The feeling of gut wrenching fear and the reality that "this just might be our last day to live", is a feeling we all experienced that day.

But, not this time, all of your survival instincts spring into action. All your training, intuition, common sense, ability and nerve kicks in at the same exact moment. I was resolved to the fact that if it was now, let it happen, but I would try and kill as many of them as I could before it does happen. We treated our wounded and flew the dead out to somewhere, then started rebuilding the hill once again.

The bunker we occupied was located about half way from the outer perimeter to the top of the hill. There was an outdoor "John" about twenty meters from our position. This was a small plywood out-house with removable half-barrels. The barrels could be taken out so the contents could be burned with diesel fuel. Using it was just barely better than "going" out in the bush.

One of the guys next to our position decided he needed to visit the head in the middle of the night, so he ventured up to the John by himself. We were to always travel in pairs anywhere we went for security reasons. He went alone. A "rock ape" attacked him. There were all kinds of wild animals over there, but the rock apes were one of the most aggressive and were not afraid of human beings. They were a little larger than a chimpanzee, but very strong.

The rock ape bit him with its long sharp fangs and bruised him up pretty bad. It also broke his left arm when they both fell off a rock cliff. We all laughed about it and thought it was funny, but he would have the last laugh. He was flown out the next morning. He didn't realize it at that moment, but he was very lucky. Any kind of a broken bone was considered a "million dollar wound".

A broken bone, of any kind, meant immediate extraction from the war zone. He was headed out of country, and maybe even back to the states. He was headed home and we were headed for Khe Sahn and more hell.

Late the next night, we killed a wild boar hog that got tangled up in our wire, and set off a bunch of trip flares we had rigged. We thought we were being attacked again from all the commotion. When the trip flares ignited, the machine gun next to us opened up and killed the boar. The hog lay out in the one hundred twenty plus temperature all the next day. It started to stink so we moved it away from our bunker. The villagers told us they wanted the hog, so we gave it to them. They ate that thing!! But the funny thing was, they invited all of our officers to the cook out to thank us for the meat.

Another Company replaced us, as security on the Rock Pile, so we headed for Khe Sahn. It was a flat plateau, completely encircled by hills of different heights. The Sea Bees and engineers had bulldozed all the trees and vegetation down and made a temporary landing strip. We never knew how long we would remain at any given place, but this area would be home for me for the rest of my time in Viet Nam.

The gooks seemed to know when a new unit was arriving, because they always sent us a welcoming gift of rockets and mortars. Since we were so close to North Viet Nam, the artillery was a lot more frequent and did considerably more damage than just the mortars in the south did. They could stay in one location and fire at will on us, because our fearless leaders and politicians back home didn't have the guts to bomb the hell out of them, or allow us to go after them. That would not have been "politically correct", or might offend some other country. Instead, our own leaders allowed them to continuously and repeatedly kill us by the hundreds.

There were three main hills overlooking the Khe Sahn Valley where the airstrip was located. They were located in strategic locations which allowed whoever controlled them to limit all activities within the entire valley below. They were known as Hill 881 North, Hill 881 South and Hill 861. These hills were so named because of their elevation above sea level.

Our Battalion (four companies) would relieve the companies on each of these three hills, plus one company would provide security for the airstrip. The plans were, once each company was assigned to a hill, we would rotate at the end of each month. That way, each company would have the assignment of guarding the airstrip at Khe Sahn every four months. This was the best of the four assignments, because there were fortified bunkers with roofs over them, temporary showers, and even a mess tent where they had hot chow twice a day!! The officers had an underground bunker where they could go when they were off duty. They even served American beer and whiskey but there was nothing like that for us.

Delta Company was chosen as the first to provide security for the airstrip and we sure were glad. It had been a long, long time since any of us had taken a shower or eaten a hot meal. It just wasn't in the cards for us. That very night, we got hit pretty hard. We had dug-in the day we arrived with our foxholes a safe distance apart, so one mortar round wouldn't kill too many of us.

The Company Commander of Bravo Company took the easy way out. He convinced the Sea Bee crew and the engineers who were there working on the airstrip to use their bulldozers and dig a long, narrow trench that would hold all of B Company. After all it was only for one night, because the next morning they would leave. As luck would have it, during the mortar attack, they took a "direct hit". A mortar round exploded directly inside the trench with them. The explosion killed the CO, the EXO (executive officer) and the first platoon sergeant. I think there were nine killed and a bunch more of them wounded. "So", they assigned Bravo Company to airstrip security and we were flown by helicopter to HILL 881 South.

While we were in the south, around Danang and in the flatlands, we went on long, lengthy patrols seeking out the enemy. Our method of operation in the north would be completely different. We primarily stayed close to the hills we occupied, and waited, because we knew the enemy was coming to us. We patrolled the areas close in around the base of our hills, so we could be sure the gooks weren't amassing an assault on us that we didn't know about.

We patroled the hills and valleys behind me. The temperature was 130° and my gear weighed over 90lbs. I am holding my mortar tube and baseplate over my shoulder.

They were intent on gaining control of these three hills, because as long as we controlled them, we could cripple their supply route to their troops in the south. The northern part of the country was a lot more mountainous and rugged than the south, which is more flat and has more rice paddies. The tunnel complexes were a lot more prevalent here, because they could dig horizontally into the hillsides and the monsoon rains didn't flood them so bad.

The tunnels, as it turned out were one of the worse experiences of my life. When we located a tunnel complex, someone had to check it our before we destroyed it with explosives. The higher echelon insisted that they needed all the information we might find inside these tunnels for intelligence reasons. I had much rather we would just blow them up with explosives and destroy any munitions hidden inside. That way, we would kill any of the enemy inside without ever seeing them.

The gooks were very small physically, so as a rule, the tunnels were very narrow and not very tall inside. I was one of the smallest men in the company in size, so guess what??? During training, we learned about all the strange, deadly creatures we would encounter in Viet Nam. One of them was called a "bamboo viper". It was a small green snake with black markings, about eighteen inches long. We were told that if one of them should bite us, we would have two choices, and only two. When bitten, we could stay really calm, sit down and smoke half of one cigarette, then die. "OR" we could get really excited, and run five steps, then die. It would be our choice. There was a bright side to all this knowledge though; the vipers didn't have fangs. Rattlesnakes have fangs that puncture or pierce your skin before they inject their venom. The vipers had small sharp rows of "teeth-like" protrusions and had to sort of chew on the skin where they bite you in order to break the skin. Then they inject venom, which attacks the nervous system. It usually took them about three seconds to break the skin, so when bitten, if we reacted really fast, and knocked them off, we just might survive a bite from one of them. Venom, which affects the nervous system, is much more deadly and affects the victims more rapidly than venom that attacks the blood stream.

When we were in an area where the gooks thought we might discover their tunnel complex, they would catch one of these snakes (or several of them) and tie a string to their tails. They would hang the snakes from the ceiling of the tunnels. Then they would tantalize the snakes until they were really mad. Our ears were the most susceptible to being bitten, because we had to remove our helmets before entering the tunnels. It was too heavy and cumbersome. The snakes could break the skin faster on our ears because they were able to "chew" on both sides of it at the same time.

I crawled through numerous tunnels in the north armed with only a .45 Caliber pistol and a flashlight. This was another time that the cold black darkness and the bone chilling fear digs into your very soul. I learned what "being alone" truly felt like down there. I knew that no one on God's earth could help me when I encountered the enemy some fifty feet below the surface, and nobody could reach me if I needed help. I never knew what was around the next corner of the tunnels. When they asked for volunteers, I did it, because I wasn't even for Dave yet. Somehow, I avoided the vipers and was never bitten, although we had some guys who were.

My hearing was destroyed as a result of the tunnels and in the old Buddhist Temple and also, from firing the mortars, but I finally got the VA to furnish me some hearing aids this year. It only took them "forty years" to admit that the roaring, ringing and lack of being able to hear all these years, was a result of Viet Nam. If you can, try to imagine firing a .45 Caliber pistol while sitting inside a refrigerator, "with the door closed"!! That would be a good comparison to firing one inside one of these tunnels.

I remember one time in particular, during one of my "excursions" into a tunnel. After I crawled out of one of them, my ears rang for three days and I could hardly hear a thing. This one was longer than normal. I encountered two of the deadly vipers suspended from the ceiling, so I was relatively certain there were gooks inside the tunnel, somewhere. I turned my flashlight off and crawled at a snails pace, listening for any faint sound ahead of me. At times, I would stop and lie still for long periods of time, and listen. The only discernable sounds I could make out were my breathing and my own heart pounding.

Finally after a long while and after crawling deeper into the tunnel, I could hear whispering voices ahead of me somewhere in the darkness. I was sure the tunnel made a turn ahead of me, but I didn't know if it turned left or right. I lay motionless for a while longer and then there was movement ahead. I decided that the tunnel made a ninety-degree turn to my right, a few feet ahead of me, and I was glad. I would have some protection. I peeped around the corner and could make out three enemy soldiers sitting inside a hollowed out spot in the tunnel. That area was quiet a bit larger and more rounded out than the tunnel where I lay. They all had AK-47 Rifles and I had only one pistol, but they had nowhere to go, because the tunnel ended where they were sitting. They couldn't get a clear shot at me because of the bend in the tunnel. When it was over and the deafening silence fell on me once more, I crawled up to their bodies and searched them for any papers, maps or anything we might use to obtain information about their plans. There were two other "Tunnel Rats" in our unit who refused to enter the tunnels after a few trips into them.

We ventured farther from our hill on one particular patrol. We discovered a small mountain lake. The water was crystal clear and clean, since it ran down the side of the rocks on the mountains. There were steep, jagged, rocky cliffs on both sides of the lake and the majestic waterfall emptying into the lake was really beautiful. The CO let us set up security, post guards around the lake and take turns going swimming in this beautiful, secluded oasis. Some of us stripped off "Butt Naked", and some of the guys dove in with their "grungy" clothes on. It didn't matter this was Heaven to us. We passed this way a couple more times and enjoyed the lake, but then, another company found out about it and got ambushed there. As you may have guessed, it was Bravo Company. They had the worst luck, but most of their luck was "self inflicted". A Platoon from Bravo Company went swimming here while on maneuvers, but they didn't post any security. The whole platoon went swimming at the same time. The gooks caught them in the swimming hole and killed nearly every one of them before we could get to them. It was "literally" like shooting fish in a barrel. Needless to say, after that, the swimming hole was off limits.

After we had been on HILL 881 South about thirty days, we rotated to HILL 881 North. It was several thousand meters closer to the DMZ and the fighting here was more fierce and happened more often. There was some sort of activity almost every night. The gooks would either make a "mock attack" on our hill, or lob a few mortars at us. Often, a sniper rifle would ring out in the night.

Anything to keep us shook up and on edge. We counted the days until it would be our turn to move to the Khe Sahn airstrip where the showers, nice bunkers and hot chow would be. Someone forgot how to count! We stayed on HILL 881 North for seventy-two days. There were no showers; we had one canteen of water per day and sometimes only one meal a day of cold c-rations. My jungle boots and trousers literally "rotted" off my body.

The hot sweltering heat during the day and the relentless cold rains at night worked on our minds as well as on our bodies. I call them "cold rains", even though the temperature was probably fifty degrees. It seemed cold to us. The temperature during the day was one hundred and thirty degrees. When the sun went down, the temperature dropped to fifty degrees in less that an hour. That is a temperature change of eighty degrees in just over an hours' time. I have stood my watch in the mortar pit many nights, wrapped in a wool army blanket. I thought I would freeze to death when it was over fifty degrees. Sounds impossible, but it happened.

We all "stank to high Heaven", but of course, some smelled worse than others, and they didn't care. I always kept a bar of soap when I could. I would go outside in the pouring rain to take a bath every chance I got. It wasn't so different from a real shower except the hot water wasn't there. Some of those guys never bathed and you could sure tell which ones didn't. As I said, our boots and trousers rotted and fell off our bodies.

We had to shave or take a bath wherever we could. This is at the edge of a small stream during one of the few "lulls-in-action".

The supply sergeant informed us that he was unable to requisition any more uniforms. He didn't know how long it would be until he might get some. We were in desperate need of more uniforms, but the really terrible thing was what we found out later. One of the pilots on a supply chopper told us that the gook civilians had huge piles of brand new military issue jungle fatigues and brand new jungle boots in the towns all along his route. They were selling them on the black market!! Our superiors knew about this and how bad we needed them, yet they did nothing about it. More Politics.

Everything stayed wet for three months during the Monsoon Seasons. It was not unusual for it to rain twenty inches in a twenty-four hour period. It seemed at times as though someone was pouring the water out of a bucket. You may have heard the story about the "Cow and the flat rock"! Anyway, there were two monsoon seasons per year and they each lasted three months. That meant that almost fifty per cent of the entire time I spent in Viet Nam, it was raining, six months out of thirteen months. It didn't just rain every day or two; it rained "every single day" (and every night) during the monsoon.

I had never in my life slept on a pillow growing up. I just didn't like to sleep on one, but I learned to over there. I had to sleep with my helmet under my head to elevate it enough to keep the water and mud out of my ears and face. Any effort to stay dry was futile. Everything was wet. Any time we stayed in one place for more than a few days at a time, I would always try to improve our living conditions. I always managed to scavenge enough materials of some kind to build a semi-dry bunker. It was dry in that the rain didn't just pour in, it sort of leaked and ran inside.

The huge rats loved the dry as much as we did. I don't know where they came from, but they were always in abundance. These things were as big as a small house cat. Hardly ever a night went by that one of them didn't run across your face or jump from a ledge in the bunker and land in your chest. Several guys were bitten and required rabies shots. The rats were plentiful everywhere we went, because there was always a trash dump where we disposed of our c-ration cans and leftovers. We killed them by the hundreds, but there was no way to kill them all. If anyone had been afraid of mice back home, they had an awful time dealing with these things running across his face while he was sound asleep.

There was a hill due west of Khe Sahn; I think it was named HILL 994. It was considerably higher and steeper than our hills. The only way to the top of it was to fly by chopper to a plateau about half way up and then scale the sheer, rocky cliffs the rest of the way. There was a squad size group of marines (eighteen of them) placed on top of this hill to gain "sight superiority" over the entire valley, including the hills we occupied. It was located only about four miles west of the airstrip, but due to the thick undergrowth, the rough terrain and rocky cliffs in between, it may as well have been a hundred miles. One night they got hit. We later determined that a full-sized Regiment of NVA troops on their way south attacked them. We guessed that the NVA had figured to over run their position and kill this small band of marines without much trouble and continue on their way. They found out that it was not going to be that easy!

The Marines on the hill contacted us by radio that they had detected probing from the enemy of "undetermined numbers". We maintained radio contact with them as long as we could. As I said, we weren't very far from the hill and we could hear the fighting with the naked ear as well as over the radio transmissions. We knew they needed our help, but there was no way we could reach them until daybreak. The fighting lasted all night long. The eighteen marines on the hill put up such a tremendous fight; the NVA thought they were being counter-attacked by a larger force. The NVA had penetrated their perimeter and the fighting escalated to hand-to-hand combat and was being fought from bunker-to-bunker. We heard, and knew the exact moment that the radioman we were in contact with, was killed.

94

At first light, as soon as we could see, we were flown to the plateau. We dismounted the choppers and began our ascent to the top of the hill, dreading what we would find. We approached the perimeter with great apprehension. A few of us entered the compound with caution and started searching for survivors. There were dead NVA everywhere. Those eighteen marines had put up one hell of a fight. A marine rose up from a bunker just beyond the communications bunker where the radioman lay dead that we had talked to. I asked him if he was okay and he said yes, but there were three wounded marines inside the next bunker. We called up the corpsman and kept looking for survivors. In all there were six dead, six wounded and six who by some wild figment of the imagination, were all right, no wounds, ("not physically")!!

Judging from my own mental status about this damn war, I can guarantee you that these kids never regained any assimilation of "normalcy" the rest of their lives. They would never "expunge" the fears and memories of that night. These were eighteen and nineteen year old boys when they left the comfort and security of their homes and joined the Marine Corps and came to Viet Nam. They had just gone through a long night of fear beyond any imagination you could ever fathom in your wildest dreams. They saw their comrades, who were like brothers killed before their very eyes, and all the time believing with all they had, that they would die too. You don't get over something like that, I know.

The tall hill in the background was where the 18 marines were the night we listened to the battle, all night. 6 dead, 6 wounded, and 6 survived. Three miles up the valley over my right shoulder was the DMZ.

Our platoon replaced them on the hill. I can't describe the feeling I had as I watched the choppers fly the last of them off the hill. Night was setting in on us. A strange feeling of the terrible occurrences that had just happened on this hill the night before was creeping into my mind. *"Would the enemy return this night to finish the job"*?? To our relief, they did not return that night. We stayed on the hill for several more days and rebuilt the bunkers and strung more wire around the top of it. We dug some new bunkers between the old ones that had been destroyed. While digging one of them, I discovered that I was digging where the previous occupants had buried their c-ration cans. I dug up a nest of centipedes. Those things were at least five times larger than the ones we had back home. They were almost an inch wide across their backs and ten inches long. They looked like a glistening black snake with bright yellow legs. Those things would have put a "world of hurt" on us, had they stung us.

This war was different from any war in history. Politicians tried to run it from behind a desk in Washington DC, instead of allowing the combat commanders to run it. They wanted us to "pacify" the civilians, yet at the same time, stay alive and kill the bad guys. Hell, we couldn't tell who the bad guys were half the time.

We received word that the VC had hit one village in particular, numerous times. Each time they entered this village, the VC would kill some of them, then kidnap and rape the young women, and take all the villagers' food. At least that is the reports we received. We traveled to this village and set up security all the way around it. No one could enter the village or leave it with out our knowing it. We checked carefully to insure that there was no VC left within the confines of the village.

Our corpsman treated the sick and diseased so called "civilians" and doctored the wounded. We gave them all the extra food we had and "pacified" them like we were supposed to do. That night, they attacked us from within the village with rifles and hand grenades! They took us completely by surprise. These were the very same people we were feeding, doctoring and protecting from the VC.

They committed a fatal error when they attacked us and killed some of us. At that point in time, we were way past the "pacification" stage of our duties. We all went a little crazier than we had already been. We killed every living thing inside the village. We even killed the dogs, and then we burned that goddamn village to the ground before collecting our dead and wounded. We retrieved them and grieved for them as we retreated back to the safety of our hill. We were under a congressional investigation for our actions, but we were defending ourselves and trying to survive. Frankly we didn't give a damn what the investigation showed, we were trying to stay alive. This was very similar to the famous "Calley Incident" they dubbed the "Mi LAI Massacre". Calley was a scapegoat for someone. He was no doubt just as justified in what he did, as we were.

Another example of not knowing whom the enemy was happened on another patrol. We were returning from a patrol, walking in a staggered column down this trail. There was an old woman carrying a bundle of straw and sticks on her back coming to meet us. A little girl was walking beside her. They were traveling toward us from our front. Nothing out of the ordinary, we met them all the time. We had already met several "civilians" on our return trip, and gave the kids all the candy from our c-rations, and were "pacifying" them as instructed to do.

When they reached a point about twenty yards in front of the man walking point in our patrol, the old woman bent over and grasped her ankles. The kid stepped around behind her. The old woman had a sixty-caliber machine gun strapped to her back. The kid started pulling the trigger. They killed eleven marines before we killed both of them. How in the hell could they expect us to fight a war like this? I thought; "how much more can we take"?? Once more, they took us by total surprise. Another one of those "lax moments".

After we killed the old woman and the girl, my mind seemed to leap back to my first night in Viet Nam, after the mortar attack. I recalled the incident when the two marines were standing beside that foxhole looking at the wounded gook. I could hear the echo of the marines' words after he killed the wounded gook, when he said, "you *will learn to understand*". He meant someday I would understand just how easy it would become to kill. I finally did, I understood what he meant. After all else that had happened to me, this was the last straw.

I felt no remorse, no regret, no pain, nothing. I felt nothing except the emptiness inside of me grow a little stronger. The rage and burning desire to kill more of them was out of control. Any last drop of pity or compassion for these people drained out of me as we filed past the two corpses and fired our last bullets into them. Not even that justified what they had done nor would it satisfy us. Now, someone had to contact these eleven men's wives, or daughters or mothers that they would never return home, and why??

I have killed and puked, I have killed and cried but I have also killed and loved every minute of it, and that scared the hell out of me. There are some who might think we were cruel, inhumane or just plain crazy, and we may have been in your eyes. Unless you were there, and witnessed the things that happened to us, you could never, ever understand. I survived Viet Nam only by "the Grace of God". He allowed me to survive and return to the real world with a small amount of my sanity left. He gave me the strength to endure, and to adjust partially; to the way things were after I got back home.

Speaking of sanity, there were many Veterans who returned home, who were not as fortunate as me. One such instance happened just three nights before we were scheduled to leave. One of the guys in the machine gun bunker next to our bunker had to take a leak. We never figured out why he went down the hill in front of our bunkers, instead of around behind them as we were

98

supposed to do. On the way back up the hill to his own bunker, he stumbled or kicked a rock or something. Anyway, he made a noise of some kind. His best buddy, whom he had been through thirteen months of hell with, woke up and thought he was a gook sneaking up on us. His buddy cut him to pieces with an M-60 machine gun. They were scheduled to leave the same time we were, in just three more days. They had made plans to visit each other's homes and meet their families. This kid literally went crazy. He lost his mind right then. We had to throw him to the ground and "hog tie" him in order to keep him from committing suicide. There is no way that this kid ever regained his sanity.

It is impossible to explain or describe the feelings or state of mind we were in after surviving thirteen months of this sort of thing. We all became something none of us wanted to be and would not have become another time, another place. Some of these kids were sent here right out of high school and had never been away from their mothers. They knew nothing about life, and some would never learn. A lot of them looked up to me because I was the "old man" of the unit. I was twenty-one years old when we left the states. I had to buy the beer when we got liberty during basic training and went into town on the weekends. These kids could not legally drink a beer before we left. As bad as that sounds, hell, they couldn't even buy a beer after they returned home! They could go over there and fight, bleed and even die for their country, but their country wouldn't let them buy a beer after they did. They weren't even allowed to vote for the ones who sent them over there.

Not everything holds such horrible memories during my tour in Viet Nam. If and when we had a few hours of slack time, we talked about home, wrote letters home and just relaxed as best we could. There were times when we would have two or three days at a time without things getting crazy. I could already throw a knife before I joined the marines, so I taught the city boys how to throw a K-Bar and make it stick every time. They loved it. If someone came up with some playing cards, we played card games. Just being able to lounge around the hilltop and relax was a luxury we weren't often afforded. At least we were up out of the muck and mud of the rice paddies, and for the moment, weren't getting shot at.

After we were in country for about seven months, J.D. and I had an opportunity to go to Taiwan on R&R (Rest & Recuperation). We had an absolute ball, but it was one of the hardest things I have ever done, when we had to climb back on that plane, knowing it was taking us back to Viet Nam. But, climb on it we did. We got to escape that nightmare for a full five days and nights. We drank a lot of cold beer and I took so many hot showers, I thought my skin would come off. It was the first time I had felt really clean in seven months. We ate all the hot food we could hold and sat at a table with chairs to eat it. The clean soft sheets were heaven. I had forgotten what it felt like to lie down on a soft, safe bed and smell the clean sheets.

We landed in Taipei, which is a city in the country of Taiwan. In fact it is the capitol of Taiwan. As soon as we checked into our hotel, we found a restaurant and ordered some hot food. When we arrived here, it was the first day of "Chinese Lunar New Years". These people celebrate this holiday by popping a lot of fireworks!! When the first string of firecrackers started popping just outside the restaurant, we hit the floor, underneath the table. We looked up at each other crouched under the table on our hands and knees. After we realized what all the commotion was, we cracked up laughing. It felt good to laugh again. It had been a long time. We had a great time for five short days and nights, but we never got use to the fireworks. I could sort of understand why some of the men who came here on R&R, never left. The statistics were staggering when they reported just how many went AWOL and didn't return to Viet Nam after being on R&R.

The fighting, killing, mental torture and fear of dying wasn't all that caused us to feel the way we did. The other things we had to contend with were almost as bad, but in a different way.

During the monsoon seasons, the torrential rains soaked us to the bone. Everything stayed soaking wet for three months at a time. C-Rations taste bad anyway, but imagine eating them with the cans half full of cold rainwater. If you can, try to imagine digging a hole in your back yard and filling it half full of water. Now try to imagine living in that hole for thirteen months while everyone around you is trying to kill you.

The insects were ruthless and the mosquitoes thrive there. They were as big as a housefly. There was a bee or a large wasp of some kind that swarmed our hill about the same time every day for a while. Those things were almost as large as a humming bird. Every day when they swarmed our hill, we would dive into the bomb craters full of muddy water to get away from them. The ones who got stung, had to be evacuated. I am deathly allergic to wasp stings, so I avoided them at all costs. There was always an abundance of scorpions, centipedes, spiders of all kinds and rats in our bunkers that we lived in. The leeches were relentless and got on us every day.

We received word that the quota for R&Rs had been filled but there was an extra one left for our company. The Company Commander called me in and recommended that I take it. There was only one available. I turned it down, because I didn't want to miss a thing. He said; "this is not a request". The pass was for four days in Tokyo and Yokohama Japan. I agreed finally to go. I wish it had been under different circumstances. The only thing I did while I was there was drink and stay in my hotel room until time to return to my unit. I did meet a marine stationed there and he took me to his camp. He was stationed at a cold weather training camp at the base of "Mount Fujiama". He showed me through the camp and we drove part of the way up Mt. Fuji. I have never regretted going on this R&R. In fact I'm glad I did. Not everyone can say they have been on Mr. Fuji. I didn't realize that the Japanese people, as a whole, still hate our guts because of WW II. But we should be the ones who hate them because of Pearl Harbor.

When I returned to Khe Sahn, I was really "short". It was almost time to go home, and I felt like I was finally ready. I left Khe Sahn in November of 1967. I wished for a long time, after I left, that I could have stayed just a few months longer. The infamous "Siege of Khe Sahn" started the month after I left, and was full blown by January and February. I think back now and realize that I believe with all my heart, that I would not have made it home if I had been there during the main Siege.

Two nights before we left for home, someone came up with some "rice whiskey". This stuff was really nasty. The gook civilians made it from rice and it tasted terrible, but man, did it have a kick. It made us feel like if we drank much of it we would "go blind". These two days I had left in country, was the "cooling off period" or rehab time they allowed us to adjust. I guess they figured that was all the time we needed to get our minds straight and to get prepared to be thrown back into society back home. We all needed help that would never come. We couldn't have gotten prepared in two years much less two days.

As I was saying, we drank the rice whiskey, but needed a little more excitement. We had no watches to stand or patrols to go on, so what the heck? I found a set of "captain's bars" somewhere and pinned them on my collar. I went down inside the officer's club, I have mentioned, where they served American beer and whiskey. I had no money, but I went anyway. Before the night was over, a full bird Colonel was buying my beer and I was rubbing him on his bald head!!! I had a ball at least for a couple of hours... That Colonel knew I was no officer, but he was a good enough man to go along with it. He knew what I had been through and that I was leaving that place. He didn't have to let it slide, but he did. I wish I could remember his name.

We left Viet Nam the day after and I will never be able to describe the feelings that surged through my mind. They were all jumbled up and so mixed up I couldn't even think straight. I stared down at this far away place through the window of the plane as

102

long as it was visible. My thoughts and prayers were of the ones who were still there. Especially for the many, many of them who would never know when they were sent home in a box.

We flew back to Okinawa and went to the huge warehouse where we left our sea bags thirteen months earlier. Somehow, it seemed much longer. As they dug through the bags and checked the nametags, they called each name out loud. Each time they called out a name and no one answered, they threw that bag aside into a pile. When all the bags had been gone through, the unclaimed pile was colossal. There were so many more unclaimed than there were claimed. They loaded them on a truck and took them away.

When we reached the states, we were granted thirty days leave. The flight schedules were all screwed up. I had to fly by way of Denver to reach Amarillo. That turned out to be a good thing. J.D.'s hometown was just sixty miles from Denver. We flew to Denver together and some of his friends picked us up at the airport. I met his parents and family. I really loved it. They treated me like part of their family, which I considered myself anyway. We had a two-day party with good old American Beer. I met all his friends and fit right in with them. Then I caught a plane on the last leg of my journey back home.

For many months and even years after I returned home and left the Marine Corps, I had a feeling of emptiness. I felt hollow and confused. I had a feeling of guilt for making it back home alive and so many had not. I also felt betrayed by my own government who sent me over there to possibly and more than likely die for a fallacy. They made us believe we were fighting to stop communism. The Vietnamese didn't care if they were in a socialistic or democratic society, they only wanted enough rice for that day and to be left alone. Our leaders had the power to end this war and stop the killing and suffering, but they chose to let it continue for their own personal gain. I hated them for not bombing North Viet Nam and destroying the French ships unloading supplies in Hai Pong Harbor. But when I got home, I hated the protestors more. They were not only protesting the war I had just returned from, they were protesting me. I felt as though they were desecrating Dave and all the brave men who died and gave these freaks the right to demonstrate and protest.

The people of this country voted one such protestor into the highest office in the land. Bill Clinton protested the war and refused to serve his country, yet he was elected Commander in Chief. That gave him the power to send more young men to die. Jane Fonda is another of our fine upstanding citizens. She went so far as to go to North Viet Nam and visited Ho Chi Minh, himself, to protest us. One of the POWs that was there when she came to Hanoi to protest, wrote his memoirs after he got home. He wrote that she is a "traitor" to this country, and I fully agree with him.

The prisoners were cleaned up and made to stand in a line to shake her hand. Their captors threatened them if they did not tell her a lie about how well they were being treated. Reportedly, some of the POWs slipped small pieces of paper into Fonda's hand with their social security number or service number scribbled on. They were desperately trying to get any information out so their families would at least know they were still alive. When she reached the end of the line of prisoners, the worthless Bitch turned to the Gook Camp Commander and gave him all the pieces of paper! The POWs, who had attempted to get the information out to their families, were beaten and starved. Some of them were beaten and tortured to death after she did that. She should have been tried for "treason".

She denies that this happened, but who is more believable, the POW who wrote it or "Hanoi Jane"? The decision is made easier when you are viewing the photo of her sitting behind the anti-aircraft gun in North Vietnam during one of her visits. She called the POWs and Vietnam Veterans war criminals that were possessed with "over active imaginations". When the Vets and POWs returned home and reported her activities, she called them "hypocrites and liars". She also broadcast anti-war jargon over the North Vietnamese radio stations, calling Americans "baby killers".

This same woman was about to be honored with more women as the "top 100 women of the century", until enough of us displayed outrage and let the stupid idiots who nominated her know what a mistake that would be. She thinks she can make everything all right by blaming her actions on being young and stupid. I agree with at least half that statement. What is wrong with the people of this country? She needs to know that "we will never forget"!

The bonds we formed with our comrades over there is impossible to describe or explain to someone who wasn't there. We all became something we had never been or would not have become under normal circumstances. Our government could have cared less about us once we had served our purpose. We were "expendable". Once we had fulfilled our obligation, they were through with us. There was no cooling off period, no readjustment time and no counseling of any kind. They discharged us and thrust us back into society. A society laden with protestors of the war and people who hated Viet Nam Veterans.

The government denied for years that multitudes of us were dying from "agent orange" and deep-seated wounds that were not visible. Some of us were dying inside for help, of any kind. They got hooked on drugs because they were unable to adapt or sort things out in their minds on their own, and our government wasn't about to help them. I was one of the very few lucky ones. With God's help, I was able to adjust, and fit back into this screwed up society. I got my life back in order after a few pretty rough years. I resisted the urge that some vets couldn't resist, so they fought back the only way they knew how. They destroyed what life they had left when they defended their rights to live here without the aggressions and malicious criticisms thrown at them. They fought back with a gun. They did what we all should have done so the government would take notice and admit that there was, in fact, a huge problem left unsolved.

A lot of the vets came home and were denied employment, because of public opinion and because they were Viet Nam Vets. The draft dodgers who ran off to Canada to avoid the draft, and refused to fight for their country, were given job priority over the Viet Nam Veterans. That made us really proud. And, to top it all off President Jimmy Carter, even granted "blanket amnesty" to all the draft-dodging cowards who left this country so they would not have to serve. Another of the things that made us proud of the people running this country.

I am proud to have fought for my country. I would do it again if they would let us fight to win. But then again, I admire a person who will stand up for what they believe in. But there is one thing you can believe with all of your heart. If you were one of the protestors who spat on us when we returned home, don't brag about it to me. If you deserted your country to avoid fighting for it, keep it to yourself. As for your rights and freedoms, believe in what you want and enjoy the freedoms I fought to defend for you, but leave me alone. Oh, and one more thing, may God help your soul if you burn a flag in front of me. Your rights will cease to exist right then and right there!

CPSIA information can be obtained
at www.ICGtesting.com
Printed in the USA
FFOW04n1205090117
31125FF